Mosley

Mosley

Nigel Jones

HAUS PUBLISHING · LONDON

First published in Great Britain in 2004 by
Haus Publishing Limited
26 Cadogan Court
Draycott Avenue
London SW3 3BX

Copyright © Nigel Jones, 2004

The moral right of the author has been asserted.

A CIP catalogue record for this book is available from the British Library

ISBN 1-904341-09-8

Printed and bound by Graphicom in Vicenza, Italy

Front cover: courtesy Topham Picturepoint
Back cover: courtesy Getty Images

CONDITIONS OF SALE
All rights reserved. No part of this publication may be reproduced, stored in a retrieval system, or transmitted in any form or by any means, electronic, mechanical, photocopying, recording or otherwise, without the prior permission of the publisher.

This book is sold subject to the condition that it shall not, by way of trade or otherwise, be lent, re-sold, hired out or otherwise circulated without the publisher's prior consent in any form of binding or cover other than that in which it is published and without a similar condition including this condition being imposed on the subsequent purchaser.

Contents

Origins	1
Man-Child	6
Call to Arms	10
Young Man in a Hurry	14
Cimmie	18
His Own Man	23
Moving to Labour	27
'Perfumed Popinjay'	32
Playboy Politician	38
The Mosley Memorandum	44
Leaving Labour	50
The New Party	57
Birth of the BUF	67
Diana	74
Grief and Guilt	78
Building the Blackshirts	83
Olympia	89
Financing Fascism	95

The German Connection – Mosley and Anti-Semitism	100
The Battle of Cable Street	109
Maginalisation of a Movement	117
'Minding Britain's Business'	125
War and Internment	130
Fascism Reborn	142
Mosley's Last Hurrah	152
An Exiled End	156
Notes	*158*
Chronology	*162*
Further Reading	*172*
Acknowledgements	*175*
Picture Sources	*176*
Index	*177*

Origins

For someone who proclaimed himself an apostle of modernism, Oswald Mosley was the product of an antiquated, indeed feudal, way of life. On both sides of his family, he was descended from prosperous Midlands squires in Staffordshire and Lancashire. Mosley was proud of his origins, and used his inherited wealth to fund his lavish lifestyle and political projects. Although he insisted that he was not a prisoner of his past, the opening sentence of his autobiography, *My Life* (1968), harks back to a mythical ancestor *Ernald, a Saxon*, before claiming English, Scottish, Irish and Norman ancestry, making him, or so he said when embracing his last political enthusiasm, a *good European*.[1]

Around 1500, the Mosley line emerged from a welter of other

Rolleston Hall

Staffordshire 'Moseleys'. 'Oswald' became the commonest Christian name for male heirs of the family. It was the first Oswald's younger brother Nicholas who became the most prominent early Mosley. Nicholas was a merchant in the cloth trade and eventually moved to London towards the end of Elizabeth I's reign, becoming Lord Mayor of the city in 1599. He was knighted the following year for his skill in wringing taxes from his fellow financiers. As a mark of her favour, the Queen also gave Nicholas a carved oak bed and a crest – the spread eagle – together with a punning family motto: *Mos Legem Regit* (Custom rules the law), or in the spin put on the tag by the 20th-century Oswald Mosley, *Our custom is above the law*.[2]

Richard Cobden

Nicholas Mosley founded the family fortune, and died clutching a sack of £400 in gold sovereigns, cursing his sons for failing to inherit his money-making skills. Before his demise, he had commissioned the most fashionable architect of the age, Inigo Jones, to build him a country seat at Hough End near Manchester.

Nicholas Mosley's son Edward, an MP, built a second house on a 400-acre estate at Rolleston near Burton-on-Trent in Staffordshire, which became the family home. Sir Edward Mosley was King Charles I's High Sheriff for Staffordshire and lent his royal master the vast sum of £20,000 to help fund the royal cause in the Civil War. The King entrusted Mosley with putting Tutbury Castle, once the prison of Mary, Queen of Scots, into a defensive posture.

A family legend told by Oswald Mosley had his gallant forebear defending Tutbury against Oliver Cromwell, who in retribution had the lead stripped from Rolleston's roof for Roundhead round shot. In fact, Edward Mosley was already a prisoner when Tutbury was taken and razed, and his lands were sequestered. Edward did not live to see the family fortunes return with the restoration of Charles II in 1660.

The Mosleys resumed the lives of gentlemen farmers into the 18th century. An ugly Georgian facade was added to the Tudor core of Rolleston, reflecting the steady accumulation of family wealth through judicious marriage settlements. The family was not tempted to return to politics until 1807, when another Sir Oswald Mosley, great-great-grandfather of our subject, became the Whig MP for the local North Staffordshire seat. On his retirement in 1837, after three decades at Westminster, the Whiggish Sir Oswald reflected that he had found in politics 'nothing but vanity and vexations of the spirit'.[3]

In the 1840s, the Mosleys, after a long legal battle, were forced to cede their ancient manorial rights to the land on which Manchester was built. (They continued to draw ground rents on their 999-year leases throughout our Oswald Mosley's lifetime, an important foundation of his vast wealth.)

The Mosleys retreated to Rolleston, where, the old house having burned down, they built an ugly Victorian pile in its place. Even by the standards of 19th-century rural England, Rolleston was a throwback to another age. The Mosleys imagined themselves at one with their tenants, masters and men. They were not above rolling up their sleeves to help

The moving force in the campaign to part the Mosleys from their manor was Richard Cobden, architect of the repeal of the Corn Laws, and the embodiment of Victorian, Liberal capitalism. He epitomised the political forces that Oswald Mosley was to spend his life battling, and it is not entirely fanciful to see the seeds of Mosley's furious contrariness in the rearguard action vainly waged by his family against the spirit of their age.

GENTLEMEN FARMERS

gather the harvest. It was, so Oswald Mosley claimed, a truly democratic community. He attributed his 'common touch' to this grounding in the rough realities of rural life. Although he lived largely in London and Paris, Mosley always saw himself as a countryman. In his dreams, at least, he might have been a happy farmer rather than a forger of the future.

In the 19th century, Rolleston's feudal fiefdom was presided over by two Mosleys. The aptly named Sir Tonman Mosley, son of the Whig MP, weighed over 20 stone and had a hole cut into his dining table to accommodate his gargantuan girth. When Tonman eventually succumbed to his appetites, he was succeeded by his son, another Oswald and the adored grandfather of our subject. This Oswald Mosley bore such a resemblance to John Bull, archetypal caricature of the stolid Briton, that he was reputed to be the actual model for this national symbol. Old Sir Oswald was a prize-winning breeder of shorthorn cattle, an authority on shire horses, and milled flour for his own wholemeal 'Standard Bread'. His organic obsessions were taken up by Alfred Harmsworth's *Daily Mail*, which promoted Mosley's Standard Bread in a *Mail* campaign.

The couple married in 1895 Mosley's mother came from similar yeoman stock. Like the Mosleys, the Heathcotes – who changed their name from Edwards in 1870 – were Staffordshire gentry. They had also returned MPs to Westminster, but in the Tory interest. Coal dug from their ancestral lands at Apeforth increased their wealth but the mines caused such pollution that the family quit Staffordshire for Market Drayton in Shropshire. Here, Katherine Maud Heathcote was born in 1874, a year after her future husband, Mosley's despised father, yet another Oswald. The couple married in 1895 and their oldest child, Oswald Ernald Mosley, was born on 16 November 1896. Two other sons, Ted and John, followed in swift succession, but when Mosley was five, his parents separated. Mosley's father cuts a shadowy figure in his son's autobiography where Mosley vaguely hints that he was weak, hedonistic and, in the last stages of his life, alcoholic.

Mosley's eldest son, the novelist Nicholas Mosley, is more honest, accusing his grandfather of 'insatiable and promiscuous sexual habits'[4] which forced Katherine Maud, a pious Christian, to leave him when she found love letters from her husband to a mistress. Katherine Maud retired to her family home in Shropshire, taking her three young sons with her. Old Sir Oswald fought his daughter-in-law's corner – staging a boxing match with his son at Rolleston, watched by open-mouthed tenants. Even with one arm tied behind his back, the old man thrashed his dissolute son. The humiliated younger Oswald installed himself at the local inn, the Spread Eagle, before taking up the life of a remittance man with chorus girls in London. His eldest son, our Mosley, stepped effortlessly into his shoes, and the unchallenged affections of his mother. As Sigmund Freud reminds us: 'A man who has been the undisputed favourite of his mother keeps for life the feeling of a conqueror.'[5] Mosley would not be a friend to Freud's race or to his doctrines, but his whole life attests to the truth of this proposition.

Man-Child

Oswald Mosley's early childhood was spent at his mother's home, Belton Hall near Market Drayton, and at Rolleston where old Sir Oswald, disgusted with his own son and heir, treated him as a son, with the added indulgence of a doting grandfather. Neither grandfather Oswald nor Katherine Maud Mosley had any intellectual interests. Their lives revolved around the traditional country pursuits of hunting, shooting and fishing. Young Oswald, who acquired the nickname 'Tom' to distinguish him from his father and grandfather, was something of a feral child in a feudal environment. *We were very close to nature,* he says in his autobiography. *I was saturated in the farming tradition . . . {and} I was glad of it.*[6] Tom tried to live up to Katherine Maud's fond names for her favourite son: he was both her 'Man-Child' and her 'Young God'.

Turn-of-the-century Staffordshire was a brutal, backward place. The customs of bear- and bull-baiting had long persisted here, and the tenants still had memories of savage encounters between dogs and maddened bulls, their nostrils stuffed full of pepper and their tails cut off. Tom's father once ordered a boxful of two dozen rats, and had his dogs worry the rodents to death while Tom and his brothers looked on. Mosley would later set great store by settling disputes with the *good clean English fist*[7] and violence followed him throughout his life. Even his most sympathetic biographer, Robert Skidelsky, admits: ' . . . there was a streak of cruelty in his character.'[8]

At age nine, Mosley was sent to a preparatory school, West

Downs, in Winchester, a 'feeder' to the ancient public school in the same Hampshire city. Young Mosley did not take to the rules governing boarding school life. The traditional recourse of adolescents at such all-male institutions was not, by his own account, attractive either: *The dreary waste of public school existence was only relieved by learning and homosexuality; at the time, I had no capacity for the former and I never had any taste for the latter.*[9]

At both West Downs and Winchester, he escaped from the boredom, the conformity and the aching cold via the gymnasium, excelling at boxing and fencing. He won the public school championships at only 15 in the foil and sabre categories. In his memoirs Mosley, noting that he was never attracted to rugby and cricket, says this was because he was used to fighting from infancy.

Mosley went up to Winchester in 1909, aged 12. He had literally outgrown his prep school; within a couple of years he had attained his full height of six foot two, a growth spurt which he blamed for his lack of academic achievement. Mosley remained an aloof loner. Contemporaries at Winchester, noted for its intellectual rigour, were unimpressed by his prowess with his pen but his skill with fist and foil kept bullies at bay. Mosley passed through Winchester like a fish gliding through water. The Edwardian public school ethos, with its muscular Christianity, missionary imperialism and belief in playing the game, barely soaked into his skin. He was his own man, from a caste born to rule, but only if he was to be the ruler.

In January 1914, Mosley arrived at Sandhurst, Britain's premier military academy. He was just 17. As an officer cadet who had only scraped into the academy by dint of six months' cramming, Mosley was expected to submit uncomplainingly to the harsh discipline. There was compensation, however: cadets were unofficially encouraged to let off steam violently in their leisure hours.

Mosley took to this regime of fighting and bullying – which he

Mosley at a Polo match at Hurlingham in 1919

later dignified with the Hellenic term *the Corinthian tradition* – like a duck to water. He recalled looking around the mess hall on his first evening at Sandhurst and, picking out *some fifty or a hundred boys who seemed particularly objectionable*,[10] deciding that these were to be his gang.

Mosley took a leading role in the buccaneering of his group. He had money via a trust fund which his grandfather had set up to stop his father drinking and whoring the family fortune away. But the younger Mosley, too, used his wealth for hedonistic ends. He bought his first car, commuting between Sandhurst and London's West End.

Like his father, many of his evenings were passed in the arms of Gaiety Girls from the Empire Music Halls, or at drunken dinners with his cronies. Having overcome an early fear of horses, Mosley also enjoyed weekend point-to-point races and polo. His passion for polo, allied to his propensity for violence, brought about the first of his many falls from grace. One weekend in June 1914, Mosley had ordered a polo pony for a match against rival army cadets at Aldershot. He arrived to find that the beast had been diverted to Wellington, and blamed his team's subsequent defeat on its absence. Humiliated, Mosley returned to Sandhurst to chastise the miscreant with a riding crop. The pony's owner promptly organised a revenge raid on Mosley's room. Attempting to escape through his window, Mosley fell 35 feet on to the ground, breaking his right ankle. The Sandhurst authorities punished the perpetrators. Fifteen cadets, including Mosley, were rusticated. But this disgrace was soon to become academic: within weeks, Europe was at war. Even half-trained officers were desperately needed. Mosley, recovered from his fracture, was eager for the fray. Here was the opportunity to achieve the glory for which his restless spirit had been looking.

Call to Arms

For a man who identified himself and his political philosophy with the First World War and the generation that fought it, Mosley, although in the fighting forces for the duration, experienced relatively little of the actual shooting war himself. This is not to suggest cowardice. Mosley would give repeated proof of his physical courage. His survival of the carnage was part of the sheer good luck surrounding his early life.

After Britain entered the war on 4 August 1914, Mosley was recalled to Sandhurst for two months of hectic training before, on 6 October, he was commissioned into an elite cavalry regiment, the 16th Lancers, based at the Curragh, outside Dublin. Mosley shared the widespread belief that the war would be over by Christmas, and, thirsty for action, he applied for a transfer to the infant Royal Flying Corps.

The RFC needed observers to spot, sketch and photograph enemy positions. It was dangerous work: statistically, RFC casualties would surpass even the murderous attrition among subalterns on the ground, and Mosley would describe the RFC as *a parade of dead men*. On hearing of the transfer, his grandfather burst into tears, crying that Tom was all he had in the world. Mosley was unable to respond. *If we had been classic Greeks we would have fallen into one another's arms in a transport of mutual emotion; I should have explained in warm and passionate words all that I felt for him; but I was just a frozen young Englishman; I could not move; I could say nothing. That has been a regret my whole life long. He died soon afterwards . . .*[11]

An aspect of the RFC that attracted Mosley was its super-elitism. He estimated that during his first few months with the corps, there were only about 60 airmen actually flying on the British side. The early aviators were seen by the public as chivalric figures from some Arthurian romance, with their dogfights and their codes of honour. Paradoxically, they were also harbingers of a mechanised future. Mosley, who prided himself both on his ancestral heritage and yet eagerly embraced technological change, was entranced.

After rapid training, Mosley found himself in Flanders by the end of 1914. He was posted to 6 Squadron, based at Bailleul near the embattled town of Ypres. Mosley's truncated training had not included actual flying. The day after he arrived, his pilot took him up for his first daily reconnaissance flight over the trenches. The squadron was flying BE2C aircraft, which Mosley characterised as *slow . . . (but) sturdy and reliable,*[12] but which Alan Clark, in his history of the air war, *Aces High*, damns as 'bad and dangerous'.[13] However, Mosley survived, which cannot be attributed to his technical skills. He cheerfully acknowledged his mechanical ineptitude, taking the lordly attitude that such things were for the *rude mechanicals*[14] on the ground – the maintenance crew – as well as admitting his inability to distinguish landmarks from the air.

The BE2C aircraft

But if Mosley lacked the essential skills of a successful airman, he did learn many lessons from the war. One was a classic Roman contempt for death: *We were like men having dinner together in a country-house party, knowing that some must soon leave us for ever; in the end, nearly all.*[15]

BATTLE OF YPRES   11

Another was an awed admiration for the German enemy. Mosley was present, observing from the ground, when the Germans attacked in April 1915 at the second Battle of Ypres. *It was an unforgettable spectacle,* Mosley recalled. *As dusk descended there appeared to our left the blue-grey masses of the Germans advancing steadily behind their lifting curtain of fire, as steadily as if they had been on the parade ground at Potsdam . . . Troops of that spirit can and will do things which most troops cannot do, and they did.*[16]

Mosley was already incubating the ideas that would govern his career: the folly and waste of war, and the overriding necessity for preventing its repetition, coupled paradoxically with the superiority of military modes over their civilian equivalents. What's more, this admiration for the German army's discipline coupled with Mosley's pride in being part of an elite formed the bones of his later fascism: contempt for democracy and civilian life; impatience with muddle and delay; desire for action and efficiency at almost any price; enjoyment of violence and the military life.

Soon afterwards, Mosley returned to Britain to take a pilot's course. Despite his technophobia, he was determined to qualify: *It is the natural desire of a back-seat driver to move to the front when it is a matter of life and death.* After four months of active service, he was already feeling *the worse for wear.*[17] He had been concussed during a forced landing, one of his legs had taken another knock, and a rest in Blighty was a welcome prospect after the nerve-shredding carnage at the front.

His damaged knee was surgically reset and after a short leave, Mosley took his pilot's course at Shoreham airport in Sussex. Training was still rushed – he had only a couple of hours of in-air instruction before his first solo flight. Yet Mosley managed to obtain his pilot's licence. However, his inexperience soon showed. Performing a celebratory flight in front of his mother, who was staying in his seaside bungalow, Mosley failed to notice that the wind had changed, made a bellyflop landing and again broke his vulnerable right leg. While recovering, he got word that his original regiment, the 16th Lancers had been severely mauled in the spring battles of 1915. Mosley limped into his medical board who, overlooking his obvious impediment, returned him to his regiment as fit.

By the late summer of 1915, he was in the trenches. The 16th Lancers were holding the line near Hazebrouck, not far south of where Mosley had been based at Bailleul. At first, front-line life was quiet, but the arrival in the trenches opposite of the Prussian Guards, the elite unit he had seen in action at Ypres, brought constant strafing and strain. In late September, a British offensive at Loos was a bloody failure, and the 16th Lancers moved in to hold the sector after the battle. Mosley's injured leg, which had not been given time to heal, was a source of constant trouble. In the rains of autumn, as he stood for long periods in the waterlogged trenches, it swelled and rotted. His Commanding officer, Colonel Eccles, informed that the young subaltern was crawling about his duties, sent him home. It was the end of Mosley's active war service, which had lasted less than six months. However, the war would continue to haunt Mosley and his contemporaries, and direct the course of his life.

Young Man in a Hurry

The Britain to which Mosley returned in March 1916 was another country. The war had ushered in a hurricane of social change. The country's young men, at first as volunteers and eventually by conscription, were being fed as cannon fodder into the trenches. Women, promised the vote at the conclusion of hostilities, were leaving home for jobs in factories or offices. The state, under Prime Minister David Lloyd George waged total war, making ever-growing inroads into the private sphere. The opportunities for a young man of Mosley's thrusting temperament were obvious.

His first task was to persuade his doctors not to amputate his right leg. They saved it, but a series of operations left it an inch and a half shorter than his left, and for the rest of his life he walked with a limp, found marching painful, and wore a built-up surgical boot. This handicap, humiliating in a fascist leader, was as far as possible kept from his followers. On recovering, Mosley joined, for the last two years of the war, first the Ministry of Munitions and then the Foreign Office.

While convalescing, Mosley had embarked on a programme of self-education. His reading ranged across history, philosophy, economics and literature. Like most autodidacts, he studied only what attracted him. He saw that society was irrevocably changing, deplored, like most of his class, the 1917 Bolshevik revolution in Russia, and was dazzled by rising American power.

Mosley was no ascetic intellectual. The props of his tripod

nature were action/violence, politics/ideas and pleasure/sex. His duties in Whitehall left him plenty of time for leisure and he plunged into the energetic social scene that a London bereft of eligible young men offered: his good looks, newly augmented by a pencil moustache; his heroic war record; aristocratic background; ready money; and the ruthlessness apparent in his dark, flashing eyes, prominent nose and cruel mouth; and, not least, his Byronic limp, made him almost irresistible to women.

He was taken up by Lady Blanche Cunard, one of the hostesses whose salons dominated London's social, political and cultural life. She introduced Mosley to the social set among whom he found the first of his many mistresses. These included Margaret Montague, a Midlands hostess who indulged his love of hunting at her Leicestershire home; and the Americans Catherine D'Erlanger and the actress Maxine Elliott. Maxine guided him into the world of politics by introducing him to Winston Churchill and F E Smith, the brilliant lawyer, wit and Tory politician who first suggested to Mosley that he should go into politics.

David Lloyd George (1863–1945) was a maverick of 20th-century British politics. An ambitious Welsh lawyer, he transformed himself from radical pro-Boer and terror of the Tories as Chancellor to patriotic wartime Prime Minister from 1916. An unprincipled, efficient pragmatist, his ruthlessness split his Liberal Party and kept it (and him) out of office after his downfall in 1922. Like Mosley, he favoured fighting unemployment and appeasing Hitler.

The Liberal chief whip, Colonel Freddie Guest, and his Tory counterpart, Sir George Younger, both asked Mosley to stand for parliament under their banners. His choice of party was not based on ideology – there was much in Lloyd George's pragmatic brand of dynamic, statist Liberalism that appealed, and the 'Welsh wizard' would eventually become one of Mosley's lasting political friends. Mosley was too impetuous and experimental to be a natural Conservative, despite springing from the Tory squirarchy. However, he accepted the Tory offer and rationalised the choice by claiming that Younger had approached him first.

He was given the choice of two safe seats: Stone, in his native Staffordshire, or Harrow, in north-west London. He chose Harrow, partly because he did not wish to depend on family connections, and partly because he wanted to be close to London. On 23 July 1918, Mosley went before the Harrow Conservative Association's selection meeting on a shortlist of four. Although his speech was unpractised and stilted, he shone in the question and answer session, and the Harrow Tories chose the tall, dark and handsome soldier as their candidate.

Mosley was selected at a decisive moment. The war was finally ending in an Allied victory. Armistice night, 11 November 1918, found the young MP-to-be in sombre mood. Entering the Ritz Hotel, the *Smooth, smug people, who had never fought or suffered, seemed to the eyes of youth – at that moment age-old with sadness, weariness or bitterness – to be eating, drinking, laughing on the graves of our companions. I stood aside from the delirious throng, silent and alone, ravaged by memory.*[18]

At the time, politics claimed all the young candidate's attention. Three days after the Armistice, Lloyd George called a general election. He was seeking a mandate for a slate of approved candidates willing to continue supporting his wartime coalition. As one such candidate, Mosley's first election manifesto is a revealing document, startling in a Tory for its lack of conservatism. Even the rosettes sported by Mosley and his supporters were the red of revolution, rather than Tory true blue.

His manifesto called for a high waged, industrially efficient society erecting tariff barriers against foreign competition. Transport, electricity and land were to be nationalised. The state would clear slums and financially support students in higher education. Immediate legislation should be passed to prevent the immigration of *undesirable aliens*[19] and promote the unity of the British Empire. The remarkable thing about this early policy statement is that Mosley adhered to its programme of state-driven economic activism and race-based nationalism for the rest of his long and turbulent political life.

Mosley's first task was to get into the House of Commons. Though the glamorous young candidate was popular, especially among the newly-enfranchised female voters, his youth and brash high-handedness also aroused resentment. One elderly Harrow Tory, a lawyer named A R Chamberlayne, stood against him, castigating Mosley for his inexperience, and even casting doubt on his military record. Mosley responded with the savage venom he always used when under political attack, threatening Chamberlayne with legal action and sarcastically apologising for *the atrocious crime of being a young man.* He slammed the solicitor as a soured representative of the *old gang*[20] who had brought about the war and learned nothing from it.

On 14 December, the votes were counted. Mosley was returned with a majority of nearly 11,000 over Chamberlayne. At only 22, he was the youngest MP in Britain. The young man in a hurry had arrived.

Cimmie

Mosley had told his constituents that he was 'the Soldier candidate' and the House of Commons was a woeful disappointment to him. The government benches, in the words of Stanley Baldwin, were packed with *hard-faced men who looked as though they had done well out of the war.*[21] The overwhelming majority were Tory businessmen determined to restore the pre-war status quo, apparently oblivious to the cataclysm of the last four years. The weak opposition was split between the rump of former Prime Minister H H Asquith's Liberals and the rising Labour Party. Mosley made common cause with the 100 or so MPs who belonged to his war generation. The press called them 'the babes'. Mosley's early speeches castigated bureaucracy and waste – one ridiculed a plan by Churchill to reintroduce red uniforms to the army in place of wartime khaki.

Mosley and his friends formed a cross-party caucus, the New Members Parliamentary Committee. There was talk of forming a new 'National', 'Progressive' or 'Centre' party to replace the reactionary Tories and moribund Liberals and head off the dangerous socialism of Labour. From the outset of his political life, Mosley was proving the bane of the whips who had lured him into politics, and an unreliable party man. Political labels were never important to him: his goal was to get things done.

In a spirit presaging the ideology-free politics of early 21st-century Britain, Mosley and many of his contemporaries were convinced that the great battles between the old shibboleths were a thing of the past. The ancient quarrels of free trade versus protectionism, even capitalism versus labour, had been blown away by the war. The problems that now confronted society were technological and scientific, only admitting of pragmatic, technocratic solutions. Mosley's particular obsession was generational. He was forever warning against the geriatric statesmen of the past and extolling young and clear-eyed arbiters of the future like himself. *Beware,* he told the League of Youth and Social Progress, a pressure group, *Lest old age steal back and rob you of the reward . . . lest the old dead men with their old dead minds embalmed in the tombs of the past creep back to dominate your new age, cleansed of their mistakes in the blood of your generation.*[22]

Lady Cynthia Curzon was the second daughter of one of the most distinguished statesmen of the age, George Nathaniel, Viscount Curzon. Cynthia's mother, Mary Leiter, the daughter of a Chicago millionaire, was one of those wealthy American heiresses celebrated in the novels of the Henry James, whom the etiolated Victorian and Edwardian English aristocracy had wooed across the Atlantic to refresh their genes and replenish their coffers.

Viscount Curzon (1859–1925) had a meteoric political and social career, most famously as Viceroy of India from 1899 to 1905. His reign in India began well, pushing through a series of progressive reforms. But after seven years, he antagonised vital figures in the Raj, notably the Indian Army commander, Lord Kitchener, with his high-handed arrogance. His reform programme blocked, Curzon resigned in a huff and came home in near-disgrace. He later served as Foreign Secretary from 1919 to 1922.

Lady Cynthia Curzon, wearing a rosette, gave Nancy Astor (right) support in her successful campaign to win the parliamentary seat of Plymouth 1919

Armed with £140,000 from her father, and with an assured income of a further £6,000 a year, Mary married Curzon in 1895. The following year their eldest daughter, Irene, was born (Mosley would have a brief fling with her before his involvement with Cimmie). Irene was followed on 23 August 1898 by Cynthia, always known as Cim, or Cimmie. The family was completed by the birth of Alexandra, known as 'Baba', in 1904. (Needless to say, Mosley would have an affair with her, too.)

In November 1919, Mosley's path crossed Cimmie's at Plymouth, where he had gone to support Nancy Astor in her successful campaign to become the first woman to take a seat in the House of Commons. Mosley, already an accomplished lady killer, had clearly marked 21-year-old Cimmie down for his own. He opened a sustained courtship campaign. At first she resisted his advances, but this only made Mosley more determined. Cimmie was well aware of her suitor's womanising. A jealous former boyfriend wrote to warn her: 'There is a reason for knowing your Tom very thoroughly, and this is best discussed with a married woman.'[23] Such dark hints may have intrigued the superficially sophisticated but actually quite sheltered Cimmie, and when Mosley lured her to Leicestershire for a hunting weekend, she succumbed.

In March 1920, Mosley came to see Curzon to ask for Cimmie's hand: 'Very young, tall, slim, dark, rather a big nose, little black moustache, rather a Jewish appearance . . .,'[24] Curzon wrote to his wife. The snobbish statesman was happy to hear that Mosley, like Cimmie, was heir to a fortune. (Mosley's beloved grandfather having died in 1916, the trustees of his estate were paying him £10,000 a year.) Since the young man was a rising star of his own Tory Party, and since Cimmie was clearly already sleeping with him, Curzon gave his consent.

The wedding of the year 1920. The Mosley's wedding was attended by the king and queen

As Foreign Secretary, Curzon gave the couple an exclusive society wedding at the Chapel Royal in St James's Palace, followed by a sumptuous reception at his official residence. King George V and Queen Mary and the King and Queen of Belgium, who had lived with the Curzons during their wartime exile, headed the list of hundreds of distinguished guests, including Bonar Law, Mosley's party leader, and the American ambassador, Walter Page. It was the social event of the season.

The newly-weds showered each other with gifts of jewels: pearls, diamonds, silver and sapphires for her; pearl studs and a gold watch for him. They departed for a honeymoon in Portofino, Italy, with congratulations ringing in their ears, including a prophecy from Curzon's former mistress, the tigerish lady novelist Elinor Glyn. 'One day,' she confidently predicted, 'you two will rule all England.'[25] To the most glamorous young couple in what was still the most powerful country in the world, it was not such an absurd notion.

His Own Man

Mosley was not the man to let such mundane matters as marriage stand in the way of his beckoning destiny. From Portofino, he proudly reported that Dante and Napoleon had stayed in the medieval fortress where they were honeymooning, and that Nietzsche had composed his masterpiece, *Thus Spake Zarathustra*, nearby – implying that he too stood in their company as an equal: soldier-statesman, and philosopher, too.

The couple returned from Italy to don their crowns as the king and queen of young London society. Their world was a round of parties and night-clubbing, racing and hunting, sporty holidays and charity functions. A Queen Anne house in Smith Square, convenient for Westminster, was their first London base. Mosley had cut his physical ties with his past. Rolleston had been sold; the big house pulled down and a swarm of villas had gone up on the land where he had grown up.

They found new country bases near Guildford and at Isfield in Sussex. Their first child, Vivien, was born in 1921, and their eldest son, Nicholas, arrived in 1923. Meanwhile, Mosley's political career had taken the first of its many dramatic turns. He continued, for a nominal Tory, to embrace a surprisingly Liberal line, particularly in international affairs. He was heavily influenced by his friendship with Lord Robert Cecil, a member of an aristocratic dynasty powerful in politics since Tudor times. Mosley pronounced his mentor *nearly a great man . . . certainly a good man; possibly as great a man as so good a man can be.*[26]

Mosley lambasted his government over a range of issues, always from a Liberal viewpoint: he criticised Britain's futile anti-Bolshevik intervention in the Russian Civil War; he lamented the lack of support for the League of Nations, which he saw as the best hope of averting another European war; he denounced the Amritsar massacre of unarmed Indians by British troops; but most persistently he nagged away at the government's repression in Ireland.

In October 1920, Mosley rose in the Commons to make the first of his attacks on the government. He accused it of carrying out the *promiscuous devastation of whole communities* reminiscent of *the pogrom of the more barbarous Slav . . . You will not restore order in Ireland*, Mosley told the front bench, *by pulling old women out of their beds and burning their houses.*[27] His interventions were greeted with sullen silence on his own side of the House; the cheers came from the Asquithian Liberal and Labour opposition.

Mosley, impetuous as ever, was quick to draw the consequences. On 3 November 1920, he crossed the floor and took his seat on the opposition benches. Sitting as an Independent, his assaults on

Despite their later political falling-out, Mosley retained a soft spot for Lord Robert Cecil (1864–1958), a fellow aristocrat. The two men shared a determination that European peace must be preserved at almost all costs. Cecil, unusually for a Tory, put his faith in the League of Nations, while Mosley, after flirting with the League, reverted to a belief in an alliance between the European powers based on common interests. Cecil's efforts won him the Nobel Peace Prize in 1937, just as the world stumbled towards the Second World War.

the government's Irish policy redoubled. On 24 November, Mosley supported a mild censure motion proposed by Asquith. The House was in an angry mood: just days before, the government's counter-intelligence organisation in Dublin had been decapitated by the IRA. Fourteen officers had been murdered in their beds by Michael Collins's gunmen early on a Sunday morning. Counter-insurgency units nicknamed the 'Blacks' and 'Tans' responded by gunning down a similar number of innocent civilians at a hurling match at Dublin's Croke Park that same afternoon.

Undaunted by the hostility around him, the 24-year-old Mosley turned the Bloody Sunday slaughter against the government, accusing them of a criminal laxness in security *which has been largely responsible for the death of many of these gallant men*. Amidst howls and catcalls he denounced the government's hypocritically unacknowledged policy of reprisals as having *obliterated the narrow, but very sacred line, which divides justice from indiscriminate revenge.*[28]

Within days of this debate, Mosley became secretary of a Peace with Ireland Council. Its members included leading Liberals such as Sir John Simon; intellectuals such as Leonard Woolf and the Catholic writers Hilaire Belloc and G K Chesterton; and socialists such as G D H Cole and Ramsay MacDonald. Armed with information gathered in Ireland by the Council, Mosley stepped up his attacks on the government's disastrous policy of half-hearted repression, even trapping the slippery Lloyd George. Mosley poured scorn on the government and its more slavish supporters. He witheringly described

Herbert Henry Asquith, 1st Earl of Oxford and Asquith, Prime Minister 1908–16

James Garvin, editor of the *Observer*, as *a musical doormat which plays 'See the Conquering Hero Come' whenever Mr Lloyd George wipes his boots upon it.*[29] In the summer of 1921, Lloyd George reached a truce with the IRA. Negotiations in London led to a treaty setting up the Irish Free State.

At the same time as these political tribulations, Mosley's personal life was in crisis. Mosley's defection from the Conservative cause had widened the breach between Cimmie and Curzon. The final break came over money. The young couple's lavish lifestyle had made inroads into even their ample means. Mosley had been attacked in his constituency's local newspaper, the *Harrow Observer*, for his stance over Ireland. Characteristically over-reacting, he responded by buying a failing rival newspaper, the *Harrow Gazette*, which he turned into a personal propaganda sheet, insisting that it print his speeches on Ireland at length. Unsurprisingly, this led to the paper's collapse, leaving Mosley with large debts. He had to sell the *Gazette* to the hated *Observer*. He was also forced to sell his hunters and polo ponies. Cimmie, for her part, claimed her share of her mother's Leiter inheritance from her selfish father. The move caused a breach between them that lasted until Curzon's death in 1925.

Cracks were also opening in the gilded facade of the Mosleys' marriage. Mosley was already systematically unfaithful to Cimmie. Under cover of his late parliamentary hours, and his assiduous attendance at the salons of political hostesses such as Ladies Cunard and Colefax, Mosley resumed womanising at a frenetic tempo. He called his trawling of the salons for compliant married women *flushing the covers*[30] – a term used for beating out game birds in rough shoots.

Moving to Labour

Mosley's alignment with Liberalism (he never actually joined the Liberal Party, though many, including the Asquiths, assumed he had) was never likely to last. His Liberal phase, (1921–23), was heavily influenced by his mentor, the 'saintly' Lord Robert Cecil.

Some observers on the left sensed that Mosley was not really one of them. The leading Fabian, Beatrice Webb, gushed in her journal: 'We have made the acquaintance of the most brilliant man in the House of Commons . . . "Here is the perfect politician who is also a perfect gentleman" said I to myself as he entered the room . . . Tall and slim, his features not too handsome to be strikingly peculiar to himself, modest yet dignified in manner, with a pleasant voice and unegotistical conversation, this young person would make his own way in the world without his adventitious advantages, which are many – birth, wealth and a beautiful aristocratic wife. He is also an accomplished orator in the old grand style, and an assiduous worker in the modern manner – keeps two secretaries at work supplying him with information, but realises that he himself has to do the thinking!' But after this lavish praise, Webb checked herself: 'So much perfection argues rottenness somewhere . . . he seems to combine great personal charm with solid qualities of character, aristocratic refinement with democratic opinions. Is there in him . . . some weak spot which will be revealed?'[31]

The Harrow Conservative Association were about, after much

probing, to place their fingers on one of Mosley's weak spots: his dishonest dissembling to suit his own purposes. Doubtless influenced by the fact that their affluent young member financed them, the Association executive had supported him after he crossed the floor. But as another election neared, their unease grew. As Mosley continued to assail the government, not only over Ireland, but on a range of economic and foreign policy points, unease hardened into certainty that he was not 'sound' on the bread and butter issues that mattered to solid, middle-class Tories.

Mosley twisted and turned, charmed and strong-armed, to keep his critics at bay for as long as he could, but eventually the executive succeeded in pinning their MP's colours to the mast of 'Progressive Conservatism'. However, Mosley insisted on adding a rider that negated all such labelling: *I cannot enter Parliament unless I am free to take any action of opposition or association, irrespective of labels, that is compatible with my principles and is conducive to their success.* Pressed to take the Tory whip, he disdainfully refused: *A gramophone would be more suitable to this requirement than a human being.*[32] Appealing over the heads of the executive to ordinary members of the Association, Mosley claimed that he had received 700 messages of support, with only 33 against.

In October 1922, the Tory backbenchers voted by 187 to 87 to withdraw from Lloyd George's coalition. 'The cabin boys have taken over the ship,'[33] sniffed F E Smith scornfully. The colourless Conservative leader, Bonar Law, at once called an election.

Mosley stood as an Independent in Harrow, opposed by a Unionist loyalist, Major Ward-Jackson. It was a dirty campaign. Ward-Jackson denounced Mosley's campaign against 'our boys'[34] in Ireland, and accused him of inciting Indian students at Cambridge University to revolt against the British Raj. Mosley sued for libel, forcing Ward-Jackson to retract and pay his legal costs of £200.

On polling day in November the voters vindicated Mosley, too: he was returned with a majority of 7,422. Nationally, the Tories remained the largest party with 345 seats, and the divided Liberals continued their steady decline. The Labour Party, however, were the major winners, doubling their number of votes and increasing their parliamentary representation from 63 MPs to 142. It was a portent for the future for Mosley, who could hardly hope to achieve his political ambitions as a party of one.

Andrew Bonar Law, Canadian-born statesman was Prime Minister 1922–23

Mosley was wooed by all sides. Lord Robert Cecil, back in the Tory Party as Minister for the League of Nations, offered him a junior ministerial job in Geneva, at the League's HQ. Asquith's Liberals assumed that the 26-year-old progressive was one of theirs. The leader himself courted Mosley at weekends at his Oxfordshire country house, the Wharf, while Sir John Simon, another leading Liberal, pronounced himself 'a great admirer'.

Mosley, however, was not to be won. Disillusioned by the League's ineffectiveness, Mosley denounced Cecil's pro-League policy as *a pyramid built on a jelly* and advocated a return to splendid isolation: *Not another dropful of British blood is to be spent in the European quarrel.* It was the baleful shadow of the trenches that most influenced Mosley. What he called his *one fundamental maxim*[35] – to avoid involvement in another war at all costs – would dictate his own stance, and that of many of his generation who had suffered in 1914–18.

In May 1923, Bonar Law, after six months in office, discovered he was suffering from inoperable throat cancer, and resigned. The battle for the succession was between the Foreign Secretary, Lord Curzon, and the Chancellor of the Exchequer, Stanley Baldwin. In the end, the King's choice was Baldwin.

In November of that year, Prime Minister Baldwin went to the country. Once again, Mosley stood as an Independent in Harrow. The themes that would become his political tunes were rehearsed in the campaign against a Tory of his own generation, Hugh Morris. Influenced by his recent reading of the economist John Maynard Keynes, Mosley advocated large-scale public works to counter the unemployment that was blighting the post-war world.

On polling day, Mosley held Harrow for a third time, but with a reduced majority of 4,646. Baldwin's appeal for protectionism

Stanley Baldwin and Ramsay Macdonald

failed, and the Tories lost a hundred seats, returning 348 members. More significantly, for the first time, Labour had overtaken the Liberals, becoming the second biggest party with 191 seats. With Asquith's support, Labour's leader Ramsay MacDonald was invited by a nervous George V to form Britain's first Labour government, a weak minority administration.

Mosley made clear where his loyalties now lay. In a slashing parliamentary attack on the defeated Tories, he branded them *a panic-stricken plutocracy* terrified of the *red bogey*. Their policy, he jeered, had been one of *drift buoyed up by drivel*. Clearly aligning himself with the new regime, Mosley portentously proclaimed that *the army of progress has struck its tents and is on the move.*[36] Just over two months later, on 27 March 1924, he formally applied to join the Labour Party.

'Perfumed Popinjay'

Mosley's decision shocked his upper class family and friends but Mosley felt he could ignore such bleats. *The battle array of the future is determined,* he informed his new party leader, Ramsay MacDonald. *You stand forth as the leader of the forces of progress in their assault upon the powers of reaction. In this grave struggle . . . I ask leave to range myself beneath your standard.*[37]

Mosley's self-confidence, and his 'calm calculation' that Labour embodied the future enabled him, as so often throughout his political life, to gloss over the negative effect his forceful personality had on others. His move to Labour had alienated two sets of class enemies: his erstwhile Tory colleagues, and some of his envious new comrades in Labour, naturally suspicious of this glamorous scion of the ruling class.

Even before his formal defection, F E Smith, the Tory who had first lured him into politics, had given him a taste of the vindictiveness to come, when he came to Harrow to denounce Mosley as 'the perfumed popinjay of scented boudoirs'.[38] Mosley wittily responded to this unsubtle dig at his notorious philandering. He did not mind about the boudoirs, he said, but he resented being called a 'popinjay', which seemed to cast doubt on his performance therein.

If his Conservative friends were appalled by his class treachery, his new party comrades were by no means unanimously enthusiastic in their welcome. Herbert Morrison and Hugh Dalton, for instance, two rising Labour politicians, deeply resented the new recruit and made no effort to hide their dislike.

However, such malice was not shared by Labour's rank and file. Egon Wertheimer, a correspondent for the German socialist newspaper *Vorwarts* saw Mosley at a public meeting in April 1924, within a month of his joining Labour: 'A young man, with the face of the . . . ruling class . . . but the gait of a Douglas Fairbanks, thrust himself through the throng to the platform, followed by a lady in heavy, costly furs. There stood Oswald Mosley . . . a new recruit to the Socialist movement at his first public meeting . . . whose later ascent was to be one of the strangest phenomena of the working class movement of the world . . .'[39]

What most surprised the German observer, was not Mosley's passionate oratory, but the cheers that greeted his wife. '"Lady Cynthia Mosley,"' whispered in my ear one of the armleted stewards who stood near me, excited; and later as though thinking he had not sufficiently impressed me, he added "Lord Curzon's daughter". His whole face beamed proudly. All around, the audience was still in an uproar . . .'[40]

The ultra-loyal Cimmie had joined her husband's switch to Labour, and predictably Mosley's mother praised his 'amazing courage and self-sacrifice'. But the couple's move attracted hostility from the Tory press which bombarded them with faux naif questions: Would they drop their titles? Why didn't they sell their properties and give the money to the poor? Why did Cimmie drip with jewels and swathe herself in furs? Absurdly, Mosley described himself as *Comrade Mosley*, brushing aside the fact that his father's imminent death from cirrhosis of the liver would make him Sir Oswald Mosley, Bart. The *Daily Mail*, always merciless in castigating the hypocrisy of the well-heeled left, caricatured Mosley in matinee idol mode at a public meeting: 'Mosley . . . caressing his miniature moustache with one hand and gaily slapping his razor-like trouser leg with the other, beamed delightedly at the girls. One of them put his titular dignity beyond all doubt by exclaiming – "Oh! Valentino!"'[41]

John Maynard Keynes (1883-1946) was an unusual economist. A Cambridge don and Apostle, he made his name outside the closed circle of the Bloomsbury set with his slashing attack on the Treaty of Versailles, *The Economic Consequences of the Peace*. His belief that the state should intervene to retrieve depressed economies influenced Mosley, F D Roosevelt's New Deal and, belatedly, post-Second World War Britain.

Mosley tried to silence critics of his frivolous lifestyle by winning his spurs in the bearpit of Labour politics. Spurning his middle-class Harrow constituents, he threw down his gauntlet in the Birmingham constituency of Ladywood, the seat of the Tory Neville Chamberlain. Mosley did not have to wait long to fight. In October 1924, the Liberals pulled the rug from under MacDonald's minority Labour government. The country was in the throes of a 'red scare' and Labour's negotiation of a trade treaty with the pariah Soviet government, as well as its refusal to prosecute J R Campbell, a Communist journalist, for sedition, played on fraying middle class nerves.

Conservatives and Liberals united in denouncing the Bolshevik bogey, and an uphill battle for Mosley *to overthrow the false Gods of reaction*[42] and a 1,554 Tory majority in Ladywood, became his first election defeat. Even so, he almost achieved an upset: the battle between him and Chamberlain went into three recounts, and at one point he was believed to have won by just two votes. In the end, however, a 77-vote majority for Chamberlain was declared.

Taking the setback philosophically, Mosley resolved to spend what he anticipated would be a short time outside Westminster in travel and consolidating his political education. Labour, losing 50 seats, returned to opposition.

Within weeks of the poll, Mosley was visiting India, where he met Gandhi and cautiously supported Indian self-government. On the return voyage he read J M Keynes's *Tract on Monetary Reform*, Keynes's work having earlier influenced his thinking when he was an Independent candidate in the election of November 1923. Always better at adapting the ideas of others than in formulating original thoughts himself, Mosley found in Keynes a framework for a constructive platform within Labour.

Mosley's reflections on Keynes, coupled with visits to the slums of the Midlands and the North during his tours of Labour constituencies, helped him to formulate his own brand of socialism – a programme which became known, from his new political base, as the 'Birmingham proposals'. In setting them out, he had the support of a new disciple, John Strachey, son of John St Loe Strachey, editor of the *Spectator*, the Conservative weekly, and a nephew of the iconoclastic literary critic Lytton Strachey. Still in his mid-20s, and a product of Eton and Oxford, John Strachey had been seduced into socialism by the Webbs, at whose salon he met Mosley. The attraction was mutual, and Mosley used his influence to secure Strachey a Birmingham parliamentary seat, Aston.

The parallels between the two men extended to their temperaments – both were coldly rational in their politics, seeking technocratic solutions to modern problems. Both were bohemian in their private lives, sexually louche and enjoying the privileges of the upbringings they had ostensibly rejected. Strachey was more deeply politically and economically educated than Mosley, and his hand is visible on every page of 'Revolution by Reason', the Keynesian tract that they wrote together.

'Revolution by Reason' arose out of a series of addresses Mosley made to Labour summer schools in 1925. The core of his message

Mosley and John Strachey

was that 19th-century laissez-faire capitalism was no longer adequate. The state had the duty to intervene in the market and manipulate money and goods to ensure full employment and increasing prosperity. Good governments would pump money into the circle of capitalist supply and demand, empowering the poor to buy, and kick-starting a stagnant economy into life. To counter inflation, Mosley proposed socialist state planning to regulate supply and demand.

One flaw in such a system was that it depended on fallible human beings to put it into practice. The idealism it embodied was shaded by a worrying seam of authoritarianism. Mosley assumed that an all-powerful state, simply by waving a wand and decreeing a new order, could reform society. This impatience with human imperfection, an inability to understand that mistakes, malice and pettiness were intrinsic to life, would stay with Mosley throughout his career. Along with his arrogance, these failures in understanding basic human nature are perhaps the most important factors in explaining his ultimate political failure. Even in the first flush of Mosley's conversion to socialism, the rhetorical seeds of fascism could be detected. They are present in the romantic language of his stirring peroration to 'Revolution by Reason'. *We stand*, he proclaimed, at a *supreme crisis* in human history. The grandiloquent phrases rolled out: *Crossroads of destiny . . . historic race . . . spirit of rapturous sacrifice . . . immortal spirit... greater spirit... awakening trumpet... magic of sacrifice... ordeal by fire.*[43]

Strachey put the finishing touches to 'Revolution by Reason' in close consultation with Mosley during a late summer holiday on the Venice Lido, one of Mosley's favourite playgrounds. Strachey prefaced the book with an extravagant dedication of allegiance: 'O.M. who may some day do the things of which we dream.'[44] They were joined in Venice by the young Tory MP, Bob Boothby, who shared their louche sexual tastes, their contempt for convention, and their impatience with the old generation and outworn party labels. Boothby recalled how Mosley, already in the mode of a lonely leader, would strike out alone from the Lido and float far away from the shore.

Playboy Politician

In early 1926, Mosley and Cimmie embarked on another fact-finding trip, this time to the US. Arriving in New York, the press treated them like visiting royalty. (Mosley reported to Strachey that he had only narrowly prevented a persistent female reporter from conducting an interview with him while he was seated on the lavatory.) They toured the city's slums, went down a Pennsylvania coal mine, and visited the Ford production lines in Detroit.

This earnest investigation of industrial and social conditions was lightened with less onerous leisure activities. They were invited to join the rising Democrat politician Franklin Delano Roosevelt on a fishing trip off Florida aboard his yacht. Mosley hunted barracuda. *Legend has it that they go for the balls and a nasty mess results,* he told Strachey. Mosley shot a passing shark with a revolver. He was impressed by the raw energy of America, but felt that Europe had the edge in being able to plan and control capitalism. Shrewdly, he identified Roosevelt's strengths and weaknesses with America's: *Too much will and too little intellect.*[45]

Returning to Britain, Mosley was engulfed by Labour politics. His progressive ideas on economics did not go down well with the class war thinking espoused by the party's old guard. The ideological opposition was mixed with bitter personal jealousy. Mosley airily swept such dislike aside. His base in Birmingham was becoming increasingly solid – helped, as in Harrow, by cash injections from his own fortune.

Although a firm opponent of Communism and fearful of disorder, Mosley stridently supported the miners against brutal wage cuts that triggered the nine-day General Strike in May 1926. It was this championing of their struggle which won him renewed popularity among Labour's rank and file and repeated election to the party's ruling National Executive.

Mosley's popularity in Birmingham made him a natural choice for the Labour seat of Smethwick in a by-election at the end of the year. But the contest, caused by the terminal illness of the sitting member, John Davison, brought down a storm of vituperation on Mosley's head. He had, it was whispered, bribed Davison into handing him the seat. Even after the National Executive had exonerated him of this smear and endorsed his candidacy, the sour Philip Snowden, a pillar of Labour orthodoxy, warned the party against making itself 'the instrument for the ambitions of wealthy men',[46] while Morrison and Dalton chimed in with their own snide assaults on Mosley's riches.

Mosley and Cimmie at Smethwick 1926

The Tory press added to the chorus of disapproval. The *Daily Mail* attacked Cimmie for wearing a dress 'dripping with diamonds'[47] – actually, as she plaintively explained, miniature mirrors on a skirt bought in India. It was widely reported that the well-born couple toured the meaner streets of Smethwick in their Rolls-Royce, and the *Daily Express* even enlisted Mosley's dying father, who charged his son with being 'born with a golden spoon in his mouth' and 'never having done a day's work in his life'.[48]

As Mosley pointed out, the venom of the Tory press was certain evidence that he was doing effective work in Labour's cause. Mosley derided the hostile journalists as *the wage slaves of capitalism*[49] and cruised towards polling day confident that the hysterical press attacks would backfire. Polling day on 21 December proved him right. He pushed Labour's majority up from 1,253 to 6,582 and even the Tory *Birmingham Post* grudgingly admitted that 'the extravagance of his opponents'[50] had helped Mosley to win.

The Mosleys had bought a rambling and charming Buckinghamshire old house, Savehay Manor Farm at Denham, near London, where their young children grew up. The parents were usually only present at weekends, and, as was common in upper-class families, the children were left largely to their own devices, the care of their loyal Nanny Higgs and a constantly changing cast of servants. The younger Mosleys do not seem to have missed their increasingly famous parents. Left to run wild, they played pirates on the river, camped out in a tumbledown estate cottage, and assumed the role of distant lookers-on when their parents entertained their friends at weekend house parties.

At the weekends, the parents entertained their eclectic set of friends drawn largely from the worlds of arts and politics. Although fervently embracing Labour, Mosley's private caresses were confined to his own class. Labour activists, with a few exceptions, he found dull and dreary company. Many of Mosley's guests and friends were homosexual – or at least bisexual – figures such as the photographer Cecil Beaton, the writer and diplomat Harold Nicolson, the aesthete Sacheverell Sitwell and the architect Clough Williams-Ellis. Their political friends tended to be Tory individualists: Churchill's acolytes Bob Boothby and Brendan Bracken, and Leslie Hore-Belisha. Holidays were spent on the French Riviera, the Venice Lido, and in the swinging centres of 1920s nightlife, Paris and Berlin.

Naively, Mosley imagined that he could keep his public and private lives separate. But in the age of a burgeoning mass media, criticism of his louche lifestyle got into the newspapers and reached Labour's more puritanical leaders. The most frequent criticisms were that Mosley was a playboy politician; a wealthy man with no comprehension of how those less privileged than himself lived. The priggish Beatrice Webb was typical of such critics: 'Deep down he is a cynic,' she wrote of Mosley. 'He will be beaten and retire'.[51]

His children saw a different Mosley. To them, he was a bewildering and sometimes alarming mixture of unpredictable tyrant and indulgent parent. He found it difficult to relate to his eldest child, his only daughter Vivien, and disguised the awkwardness behind a barrage of banter that too easily shaded into cruel taunting that permanently marred their relationship.

His eldest son, Nicholas, has left a telling portrait of his father through the eyes of an intelligent and curious child. In awe of Mosley, Nicholas recalls him at one moment 'roaring' in incendiary rage at some frustration or unfortunate servant. At other times, wilfully eccentric – Mosley liked to wander round his rose garden stark naked composing his speeches – there was always a cruel edge to his continual teasing and love of practical jokes. He once served an omelette stuffed with tobacco to an unwelcome guest.

His behaviour could be terrifying. Irritated by the barking of his children's dog, he discharged both barrels of a shotgun from his study window at the animal. His rudeness to servants – especially men – meant that few stayed long. At other times, especially at Christmas, he played the paternal role with energy and touching dedication, spending hours on elaborately disguising himself as Santa Claus before lavishing gifts on his offspring, whom he fondly addressed as *young porkers*.[52]

The image of upper-class dilettantism which Mosley made little effort to counter was only partially accurate. He worked hard in Labour's cause. If his weekends were passed partying with his glitzy friends, his weeks and evenings were spent working for the party. He made serious speeches on economics to a half-empty Commons, and toured the country addressing local Labour Party meetings. His efforts won the respect of some of the most ardently left-wing leaders of the Labour movement such as James Maxton, leader of the Independent Labour Party, and Arthur Cook, the militant miners' leader. In contrast to Mosley's middle-class Labour enemies, these working class socialists took Mosley at his own evaluation. Above all, he won golden opinions from Labour's leader, James Ramsay MacDonald, a working-class Scot susceptible to the charms of the English aristocracy.

> James Ramsay MacDonald (1866–1937) was Labour's first Prime Minister. A working-class Scot who opposed the First World War, he formed a minority government in 1924 and was returned to Downing Street in 1929 with a majority. By then, the principled firebrand had become a cautious, bumbling buffoon, more at home in the company of aristocrats such as Mosley than his former party comrades.

An example of Mosley's double life came in the late summer and early autumn of 1928 when he spent weeks holidaying at Antibes on the French Riviera with Douglas Fairbanks, Somerset Maugham, Boothby, Strachey, and his mistress Georgia Sitwell, much to a mortified Cimmie's misery. Swimming and flirting by day, casino gambling and love-making by night, enjoying the bequest of jewels that he had inherited – along with the baronetcy – from his recently deceased father, Mosley acted out the role of the playboy to its fullest. To his brother Ted's disgust, he refused to interrupt his vacation to visit his father's deathbed. He did, however, attend the funeral. Within weeks of this hedonistic holiday, he was touring central Europe with MacDonald, introducing the leader to the politics of Austria, Germany and Czechoslovakia.

As the 1920s drew to a close, Mosley seemed suspended between two worlds. He was fun-loving, contemptuous of others' opinions and deeply cynical in his private life but also, in his political life, idealistic, interested in ideas, courageous, energetic and moved by the waste and suffering caused by war and unemployment. The long weekends at Denham, the acting-up in front of new-fangled ciné cameras; were matched by the Mosleys' hospitality to working class Labour supporters from Birmingham, when the great barn at Denham and the 120-acre estate were thrown open to the jobless and the party faithful. These tensions between the contrasting poles of Mosley's personality would determine the course of his life over the next decade and beyond.

Sacheverell and Georgia Sitwell

The Mosley Memorandum

In May 1929, Conservative Prime Minister Stanley Baldwin called a General Election. The main campaign issue was the growing scourge of unemployment, with industrial and commercial stagnation laying waste to broad swathes of Scotland, Wales, the Midlands and the North. Baldwin led the Tories under the uninspiring slogan: 'Safety First'.

Labour, while promising to improve the lot of its working class supporters, was vague about how this was to be achieved. Nor was the staid and timid party leadership, under dim luminaries such as MacDonald, Philip Snowden, Arthur Henderson and J H Thomas, about to usher in a British revolution. Only the Liberals, under Lloyd George, offered coherent proposals to combat unemployment. With the intellectual input of Keynes, they proposed a programme of public works financed by loans to reinvigorate the economy. Such ideas were much more in tune with Mosley's thinking than Labour's rhetoric, but the Liberals' hour had passed.

With his habitual energy and enthusiasm, Mosley threw himself into the campaign. Mosley money was recklessly flung into financing the campaigns of his less well-off local comrades, including John Strachey, standing at Aston, and Allan Young, running in Ladywood. Mosley's eyes were also on the campaign of another Labour candidate: Cimmie had been chosen as the candidate for Stoke-on-Trent, near Mosley's ancestral lands in Staffordshire, and Mosley affected to be worried that his wife's majority would eclipse his own in Smethwick.

On election night, Cimmie's majority did indeed exceed his – she won by 7,850 to his 7,340. In Birmingham, six city seats fell to Labour as the Conservatives crumbled. For the first time, Labour were the largest party in the country – winning 287 seats to the Tories' 261. The Liberals, for all their intellectual coherence, were reduced to a rump of 59. For the second time, Labour, led by a more cautious than ever Ramsay MacDonald, were in office, if hardly in power.

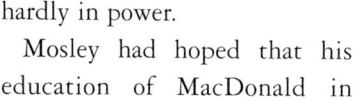

Cimmie Mosley 1928

Mosley had hoped that his education of MacDonald in European affairs would win him the Foreign Office, but he was disappointed. His reward was the Chancellorship of the Duchy of Lancaster – a minister without portfolio, outside the Cabinet but with a special brief to combat unemployment. Unfortunately, his dynamism was dragged down by the conservatism of his ministerial superiors: the septuagenerian former railwayman's leader J H Thomas; the elderly pacifist George Lansbury; and the Treasury official assigned to be Mosley's secretary/minder, the former Fabian, Dudley Ward, who was notable for his dull conservatism.

At the end of July, Mosley had addressed the Durham Miners' Gala. Flattering his audience by describing them in fascist terms as *the stormtroops of Labour,* Mosley concluded: *I would rather see the Labour Government go down in defeat than shrink from great issues . . .*[53]

But Mosley soon discovered that shrinking from great issues was what the MacDonald government was all about. As a brash young minister, anxious for action to achieve real reforms, Mosley found he was banging his head against a brick wall.

During the August holidays in 1929, the Mosleys went for their customary long vacation to Antibes on the French Riviera, along with Cimmie's sisters Irene and Baba. Here, Mosley's increasing curtness towards his wife was again on blatant display. He ignored her while pursuing his latest mistress, the model Paula Casa Maury. Outraged by Mosley's cruelty, Irene called him 'a cad'. Earlier she had recorded in her diary: 'She [Cimmie] is so exquisite and faithful in her love and he so ruthless with her. I wish at times he could disappear off the face of the earth as he only brings her endless agony.'[54]

Nevertheless, there were underlying strengths in the Mosley marriage that kept it going. The couple wrote affectionate long letters to each other in the baby language favoured by the English upper classes (he was 'Tommy' and she was 'Timmy'). Mosley was occasionally touched by remorse for his unfaithfulness, managing to convince himself that their love excused his behaviour. Cimmie still adored Mosley and begged him to become once more the loving man for whom she had first fallen. But Mosley was quite unable to meet these expectations, even if he had been willing to try.

Returning from the summer recess, and taking seriously his brief to come up with ideas to fight unemployment, Mosley advocated increasing old age pensions to encourage early retirement, making room for young people to enter the jobs market. In December, the Cabinet rejected the scheme. Undaunted, Mosley's next proposed a Keynesian public works scheme: raising a loan to finance his road-building programme. But faced with the implacable opposition of Philip Snowden's Treasury, this too was a non-starter. What's more, Snowden was backed by the Minister of Transport, Herbert Morrison, another of Mosley's long-standing foes, and by Mosley's own boss, J H Thomas, who, as a railwayman, was not anxious to promote rival roads.

Mosley may have imagined that his wooing of MacDonald during Denham weekends would give him enough leverage with the Prime Minister to overrule Snowden. But, as usual, Mosley had overestimated his influence. MacDonald was no economist, and like the other Labour leaders, was no longer a socialist either. Entranced by the trappings of office and the embrace of the aristocratic establishment, he would not alarm his rich friends by offending orthodoxy. Kept firmly in line by Snowden, MacDonald's priority was to avoid rocking the boat. By this time, the inherent weakness of his position in the government had finally dawned on Mosley: he held office, but was without power.

Philip Snowden (1864–1937) MacDonald's Chancellor of the Exchequer, was a dedicated follower of financial orthodoxy, and a bitter personal enemy of Mosley. State intervention smacked to Snowden of socialist adventurism. He clung to the traditional doctrines of free trade, set against protectionist moves to shield the home market from the gathering storm of worldwide recession.

At the start of 1930, the future was looking distinctly ominous. The previous October had seen the Wall Street Crash, and the world's economy started to slide into the Great Depression. In this climate, the government's only coherent economic policy – to stimulate trade – lay in ruins. By March, with unemployment climbing to 1,700,000, even MacDonald admitted that the world was rocking in an 'economic blizzard' – to which no-one seemed to have an answer. Among Labour's ministers, only Mosley seemed confident that unemployment could be conquered.

But Mosley was unable to shake his colleagues out of their paralysis. As Beatrice Webb noted in her diary: 'Mosley . . . is contemptuous of Thomas's incapacity, of the infirmity of manual working Cabinet Ministers generally, and very complacent about his own qualifications for the leadership of the Labour Party. That young man has too much aristocratic insolence in his make-up.'[55]

Mosley had spent the Christmas recess working on his proposals for meeting the crisis. This 15-page document, the 'Mosley Memorandum', embodied perhaps the most radical economic proposals ever laid before a British government. By the time Mosley sent it to the Prime Minister in late January, it had already been approved by Keynes himself. Couched in a modest, moderate style, designed to appeal to his cautious seniors, Mosley's proposals pointed out that unemployment was becoming so grave that tried and tested economic orthodoxies had to be set aside to deal with it. Drastic solutions were the only answer.

The Mosley Memorandum reiterated his suggestions for early retirement pensions and a publicly-funded road-building scheme. In addition, it recommended the setting up of a government-controlled industrial bank to channel funds into work-creation schemes. Mosley also proposed a small inner Cabinet modelled on Lloyd George's all-powerful 1917 War Cabinet. Chaired by the Prime Minister, this body of half a dozen ministers would possess almost military powers to direct the fight against unemployment.

Although Mosley's ideas were very similar to the New Deal policies that President Roosevelt would shortly introduce in the US, they proved altogether too much for the MacDonald government. The Prime Minister hid behind protocol to avoid facing up to the problems that Mosley had rightly highlighted. A befuddled Thomas, irritated that Mosley had not shown him the 'Memorandum' before sending it to MacDonald and desperate to escape responsibility for the crisis, offered his resignation. At the same time, John Strachey, Mosley's Parliamentary Private Secretary, left the 'Memorandum' lying around in his house while journalists were present. As a result of this, the 'Memorandum' burst into the public domain. MacDonald, nettled and feeling himself put under pressure by Mosley, characteristically tried to kick the 'Memorandum' into the long grass by appointing a Cabinet sub-committee to consider it.

While the sub-committee ruminated, Mosley's enemies in the party stepped up their attacks. Snowden patronisingly called him a 'young man',[56] while Morrison complained that Mosley spoke 'like a landlord addressing his peasantry'.[57] With characteristic impatience, Mosley began to talk of resigning. Rumours of his intentions reached his friends – Harold Nicolson noted them in his diary as early as January 1930 – and by mid-March they were deafening.

Bob Boothby wrote Mosley a wise letter, counselling him to ride out the storm. Boothby pointed out that Mosley had burned his bridges with the Tories, but had too many enemies within Labour to take over that party now. As Mosley was 'the ONLY one' capable of translating into action the ideas of the post-war generation, Boothby advised him to accept defeat over the 'Memorandum' until events wafted him to power presiding over 'a moderate government of the Left'.[58] Sage counsel, but the tragic flaws of Mosley's character prevented him from heeding it.

Leaving Labour

Through the spring of 1930, debate over the 'Mosley Memorandum' raged on in the press and within Labour's ranks. Mosley received powerful backing from left-wing publications such as the *New Statesman*, and 80 Labour backbenchers demanded that the proposals should at least be publicly discussed. The 'Memorandum' itself was being passed from committee to sub-committee behind the closed doors of Whitehall.

Finally losing patience, Mosley demanded a meeting with MacDonald on May 19th at which, the prime minister complained, he was 'on the verge of being offensively vain'. The next day, Mosley resigned from the government in a letter described by MacDonald as 'gracelessly pompous'.[59]

Mosley was clear about his reasons for going. It came down to MacDonald having to choose between the action he proposed, or the inaction propounded by Snowden and the Treasury. But MacDonald had retreated into procrastination. Not for the first or the last time, a weak Prime Minister was in thrall to a tough-minded Chancellor. Even if it meant giving up his agreeable weekends at Denham, MacDonald offered Mosley up as the sacrificial scapegoat for Labour's and his own confused failings.

Mosley was still subject to illusions. He believed that he could beat the government by appealing over the heads of ministers to the Labour faithful at large. But as Bob Boothby regretfully reminded him, given his capacity for upsetting apple carts and making enemies, 'the cumulative effect of so many hostile forces would overwhelm Napoleon himself'.[60]

Unfazed, Mosley lost no time carrying his campaign to the country. Within 48 hours of his resignation, he addressed his fellow MPs in the parliamentary Labour Party, advocating a vote of censure against the government for not acting on the Memorandum. When Mosley put his motion to the vote, the result was humiliation: party discipline prevailed and Mosley's motion was defeated by 210 votes to 29. He was discovering that his own gifts – passion, rhetoric, idealism, flexibility of mind – were no match for habit, or threats to political careers.

Nevertheless, this was Mosley's moment, the only time a lifetime of sailing against the political tide when press and public opinion, and the sympathy of many intelligent and far-sighted political peers was clearly behind him. Sympathy for Mosley united friends such as Boothby, Strachey and Harold Nicolson, and also future political stars such as Aneurin Bevan, the fiery Welsh spokesman of Labour's left-wing, and Harold Macmillan, a progressive Tory of Mosley's war generation. Macmillan, a future Prime Minister, wrote to *The Times* commending Mosley's principled resignation: 'I hope some of my friends will have the courage to support and applaud his protest.'[61]

Among Tories, besides Boothby and Macmillan, Oliver Stanley, Walter Elliott and Henry Mond backed him, while from the Liberals Archibald Sinclair and Leslie Hore-Belisha lent their support. It should be noted, in view of Mosley's later anti-Semitism, that two of these backers – Mond and Hore-Belisha – were Jewish. Nevertheless, there were distinctly fascist undertones in the salons where Mosley's sympathisers gathered in the summer of 1930, as unemployment figures reached two million, and the government dithered and drifted.

But beyond the interest and sympathy there also ran deep distrust. If Mosley's limited patience with Labour ran out, as it had with the Tories – where would his journey end? Did this impatience not indicate instability, vanity and arrogance – the fatal trinity of faults that had dogged Mosley throughout his whole political career?

Anticipating the charges of treachery that would be thrown at him by his former party comrades if he left Labour, Mosley began to chart a new political landscape. No longer, he told readers of the *Sunday Express*, would political divides run along the faultlines of class and party. A new chasm had opened up between the generations. *Modern man . . . is a hard, realistic type, hammered into existence on the anvil of great ordeal. In mind and spirit he is much further away from the pre-war man than he is from the ancient Roman . . . The types which have emerged from the pre-war and post-war periods are so different that they can scarcely understand each others' language.*[62]

Consciously or not, Mosley's language and ideas – his contempt for the 'old gangs' – reflected the thinking of fascists in continental Europe. Such movements had been carrying all before them since Benito Mussolini's Italian Blackshirts had seized power in 1922, the year that had seen the fall of Lloyd George's dynamic coalition in Britain, and the return of the dead-headed party politics of Baldwin and MacDonald. Ranged against such withered representatives of the old gangs, claimed Mosley, was youth – the war generation – who had earned the right to govern by the blood sacrifice they had made in Flanders.

In 1919, the Italian fascist Benito Mussolini (1883–1945) formed the Fasci di Combattimenti from a pool of ex-servicemen in Milan, and by October 1922 had taken power. The 'Duce's' dictatorship and leadership cult, much admired abroad despite its repressive brutality, lost support and direction when its foreign adventures floundered in Abyssinia and Albania. Mussolini's ill-judged alliance with Hitler's Germany finally spelled his end.

Influenced by covert conversations with younger Conservatives

Prime Minister Neville Chamberlain fixing the attention of Benito Mussolini

and his own Labour followers, Mosley decided on a last throw of the dice within the old party system. He would appeal to the Labour rank and file at the party's annual conference in Llandudno in October 1930. In a short speech lasting barely 15 minutes, Mosley outlined his manifesto. The Labour government should force banks to invest in reconstruction. Britain's home markets must be insulated from global depression behind tariff walls. An action programme must stimulate work and demand. Above all, Labour should not shrink from the challenge – but seize it and lead the country out of the shadows. A left-winger, Fenner Brockway, described the reception of Mosley's speech as the greatest ovation he had ever heard at a party conference. Even the ultra-Tory *Morning Post* described Mosley as the 'Moses' who might yet lead Labour out of the wilderness. When it came to a vote, however, the undemocratic system of trade union block votes, under which union barons cast notional ballots on behalf of thousands of their unconsulted members, crushed Mosley's motion.

Even now, Mosley had still not quite given up on Labour – two days later, sharing a Merseyside platform with the transport union boss Ernest Bevin, he used fascist imagery to call for *an iron spirit and an iron will*[63] in an age of iron to cut a path through to victory. He was cheered to the rafters. For the rest of the year, Mosley continued to speak at Labour meetings while wooing disaffected Tories and Liberals. John Strachey, Aneurin Bevan and Allan Young composed a new document, the 'Mosley Manifesto', restating the case for a small emergency Cabinet, public works and protectionism towards home industries. Strachey pointed out that it was no good arguing about the ownership of industry when very soon there would be no industry left. The Manifesto was to be the programme for a ginger group, the 'New Labour Group' which would fight for Mosley's policies to be adopted by the government. The 17 signatories of the Manifesto included Bevan, Oliver Baldwin, Strachey, W J Brown, Robert Forgan and the Mosleys themselves. All were young, half were from the Black Country in and around Birmingham, and most represented working-class constituencies hit by the Depression. The miners' union secretary, Arthur Cook, also signed the Manifesto.

But beneath all this Labourism, the whiff of fascism was in the air. Mosley, as his biographer Robert Skidelsky records, was already in the mood to take 'the first tentative steps that were to lead him to fascism'.[64] Perceptively, the *Punch* cartoonist, Bernard Partridge, recognised where Mosley's march was leading. In a cartoon captioned 'MOSLINI' he depicted Mosley carrying a banner proclaiming 'The Mosley Manifesto wants a National cabinet of Five'. Mosley is accosted by Mussolini, who protests: 'Five dictators! Why worry about the other four?'[65]

As Mosley basked in a warm glow of popular approval, Tory friends such as Boothby, Macmillan and Walter Elliott fired off letters of support to the press. Harold Nicolson devoted a BBC radio broadcast to praising his friend's boldness, while J R Garvin, right-wing editor of the *Observer,* forgetting the young Mosley's description of him as 'a musical doormat,' lauded his 'brilliant fearlessness'.[66]

There was support of a more tangible kind from the motor car tycoon Sir William Morris. After calling for the formation of 'an Industrial party', and 'strong government' under a 'real leader' Morris decided that Mosley represented the 'ray of hope'[67] that the country needed. In January 1931, Morris handed Mosley a cheque for £50,000, specifically earmarked to launch a new party. But the gift came with a warning that further support would depend on Mosley's sustained success. Big business – and particularly heavy industry mass-production tycoons like Krupp, Thyssen and Siemens in Germany, Ford in the US and Renault in France, supported fascist movements as a counterweight to Communism, and a useful means of 'disciplining' their own work forces and restoring the stability on which their profits depended.

Mosley's difficulties, as he prepared his leap into the political unknown, were formidable: he was up against vastly powerful vested interests, political machines that kept their members – particularly in Labour – in tight thrall. Well aware of the power of habit, coercion and tradition, Mosley, as he had done in Harrow when leaving the Tories, dissimulated and deceived his loyal local party in Smethwick, which had hitherto supported his stand against the Labour leadership. As late as January, he assured his constituency party officials that he had no intention of leaving. But with Morris's cheque in the bank he took the plunge. In the end, only five fellow Labour MPs took the brave decision to resign with him: Cimmie, Strachey, W J Brown, Robert Forgan and Oliver Baldwin. Bevan did not join them. Prophetically, he warned Mosley: 'Where is the money coming from? . . . You will end up as a fascist party.'[68]

With an eye to publicity, the Mosley rebels had agreed to resign in a staggered series. The first scheduled departee, Brown, got cold feet when the union that sponsored him threatened to withdraw its financial support. Mosley, who had been stricken at this critical juncture with pleurisy and double pneumonia, was driven round to Brown's home on a stretcher in a vain effort to shame him into keeping his word. All the other resignations went ahead, amidst much bitter recrimination from Labour loyalists. Labour did not wait until Mosley himself quit. On 10 March 1931, he was expelled from the party for 'gross disloyalty'.[69] A fortnight before, symbolically at the same Farringdon Road meeting hall where the Labour Party had been born three decades before, Cimmie Mosley, deputising for her sick husband, and supported by Strachey and Oliver Baldwin, officially launched the New Party.

The New Party

In the early 1930s, the British political scene was fluid. The Depression had unnerved the most staid and conservative figures, and traditional party political ties had loosened and blurred. The press lords whose support Mosley hoped to win were contemplating launching a party of their own. Lord Beaverbrook, who lent Mosley his home on the Riviera to recuperate from his illness, had put up a candidate in a by-election on a platform of empire loyalism. Churchill had quit the Tory front bench over his opposition to Indian independence. The much-riven Liberals had just split again, with Sir John Simon leading a dozen rebels in opposition to Lloyd George's radicalism. Another politician, Leslie Hore-Belisha, contemplated leading yet another rebel Liberal group into Mosley's ranks.

Only one Tory MP, the wealthy Ulsterman W E D Allen, had defected to the New Party – and he subsequently proved to be an agent of the security service MI5, deputed to report on Mosley. Still, he was able to recruit a few Labour activists. Socially prominent recruits proved more elusive, but some signed up, motivated by personal admiration for Mosley and a belief that only his radical plans offered a way out of what increasingly looked like a terminal crisis of capitalism. The most well-known was Harold Nicolson, diplomat, historian, journalist, broadcaster, politician and socialite whose diaries recorded the brief life of the New Party. Another intellectual supporter was C E M Joad, pacifist, Labour philosopher and future mainstay of the popular *Brains Trust* radio programme.

Party meetings attracted curious crowds, but also drew left-wing militants determined to strangle the New Party at birth. The party's meetings were broken up by organised Communist and Labour hecklers, and Mosley determined to set up his own party militia to protect meetings and intimidate would-be troublemakers. This defence squad, informally known as the 'Biff Boys', and composed mainly of upper-class Oxbridge hearties, was led by Peter Howard, England rugby captain, later a *Daily Express* journalist, and propagandist for the right-wing revivalist Moral Re-Armament movement.

The 'Biff Boys' were the germ of Mosley's fascist Blackshirt toughs, and similar strong-arm squads were used by all Europe's fascist movements. Mosley justified them by the need to guarantee 'free speech' at his meetings, but increasingly the line between defensive and offensive behaviour became hazy, and the activities of the 'Biff Boys' were glaringly at odds with the marigold that the New Party had chosen as its emblem.

The party's first big test was a by-election at Ashton-under-Lyme in Lancashire, a depressed cotton town where nearly half the workforce was unemployed. Within six weeks of its foundation, the New Party descended. It was still *Hamlet* without the prince, since Mosley himself was still convalescent. The party's candidate was Allan Young, Mosley's former agent, supported by the distinctly upper-class team of Cimmie, Strachey, Nicolson, Joad and a dozen Biff Boys in plus fours.

Mosley's arrival barely a week before polling day set the damp campaign alight. Two meetings each attracted audiences of more than 7,000, and Nicolson memorably portrayed Mosley, prowling the platform like a panther, jabbing an accusing finger at his mesmerised audience.

Labour was worried enough to draft in a battery of party big guns in an effort to blow the New Party out of the water. Labour's bitter rhetoric against Mosley knew no bounds. A V Alexander called him 'traitorous'; Emmanuel Shinwell a 'Brutus'; and Arthur Greenwood referred to him as 'the first rat to leave a ship he thought was sinking'.[70]

The vicious epithets were justified in Labour's eyes by the result of the Ashton by-election: Tories: 12,240; Labour: 11,005; New Party: 4,472. A Labour majority of more than 4,000 had been converted into a Tory one of more than a thousand, handing the Conservatives a natural northern working-class Labour seat. The intervention of the New Party was held responsible and a howling mob gathered outside Ashton Town Hall, where the count was held, to hurl abuse at Mosley, Cimmie, Strachey and Allan Young. As he contemptuously surveyed the mob from the steps, with cries of 'Judas', and 'Traitor' echoing in his ears, Mosley turned to Strachey and hissed: *That is the crowd that has prevented anyone from doing anything in England since the war.*[71]

'At that moment,' Strachey remarked later, 'British fascism was born: at that moment of passion, and of some personal danger,

Mosley with his Blackshirts, William Joyce stands on the left.

Mosley found himself symbolically aligned against the workers.' Mosley's arrogant self-righteousness had curdled into contempt for the ordinary Labour supporters who had carried him so far.

Finding himself undergoing the novel (but soon to be familiar) experience of defying a hostile mob, Mosley acted with courage and chivalry: he smuggled Cimmie out of the Town Hall's back door, and then, his face 'white with rage not fear'[72] and with a thin smile on his lips, he led his group through the chanting crowd to safety.

Over the summer, the New Party leadership took stock of its disastrous electoral debut. The party's executive council met daily in its London offices in Great George Street and gathered for weekends at Denham. Quickly, divisions surfaced. Strachey and Young were determined that the party should adopt Marxist-socialist solutions to the crisis. Joad and Nicolson fretted about the violence of the Biff Boys. Mosley himself seemed increasingly attracted by fascism – speaking 'soulfully' about the corporate state of the future. Speaking at the Cannon Street Hotel in the City of London on 30 June 1931, he told business leaders, using fascist rhetoric, that the New Party sought to create *a new political psychology, a conception of national renaissance, of new mankind and of vigour.*[73]

Strachey was alarmed by what he heard. The next day he warned the New Party's Youth Movement against political violence. His remarks were reported in the Labour *Daily Herald* in a way which made them look like a rebuff to Mosley. An angry Mosley called his first lieutenant to order at the next meeting of the party executive.

Mosley was fighting several battles simultaneously. As he strove to keep an increasingly unhappy Strachey and Joad on board, he was facing an organised attempt to stifle his party. The political establishment was determined that the New Party should not be allowed to shatter the cosy consensus of British party politics.

Strachey claimed that political correspondents had been briefed not to mention the New Party, while the BBC pulled a radio debate between Mosley and a Tory peer without explanation. On the left, socialist militants continued to break up New Party public meetings in a deliberate and largely successful attempt to prevent it getting its message across. All of these factors were pushing Mosley in a direction to which he was increasingly inclined: fascism.

Mosley was continuing his contacts with influential figures outside the party in preparation for the economic crash that he remained convinced was coming. He sought support via two doyennes of London's social scene: Lady Houston, owner of the magazine *Time & Tide*; and Lady Sybil Colefax, who was asked to canvass party subscriptions from wealthy guests at her salons. Over the weekend of 21/22 July, Mosley met the two disaffected giants of British politics, Churchill and Lloyd George, at the home of the Liberal leader Archibald Sinclair. Lloyd George proposed that they form a National Opposition to the coming National Government coalition between Baldwin and MacDonald. But this promising moment passed, and that very day Mosley was faced by the gravest crisis of the New Party's short life.

On 22 July, Strachey, who had engineered his inevitable showdown with Mosley by proposing (ludicrously) that Britain should cut its ties with the Empire, the US and France in favour of a close military and political alliance with the Soviet Union, resigned from the New Party along with Allan Young. Two days later, Joad followed them. All three cited what Joad called 'the cloven hoof of fascism' which they had detected in the party. The New Party, jibed Joad, was about to 'subordinate intelligence to muscular bands of young men'.[74]

Mosley did his best to ignore the negative impact of these resignations. At the end of July, he addressed a mass rally of 40,000 people in Derbyshire, declaring: *We invite you to something new; something dangerous.*[75]

Something dangerous was already afoot. The economic storm which had been gathering all summer burst. The May Committee, set up to examine the effects of the Wall Street Crash on the British economy, reported that a budget deficit expected to be £20 million would in fact be closer to £170 million. May recommended an across-the-board slashing of government spending: salaries of all state employees, from ministers to civil servants and servicemen, should be cut. The brunt of the cuts, however, would be borne by the growing army of the unemployed, who would have their already meagre benefits slashed by 20 per cent. This alone would make up £67 million from the total savings of £97 million that May deemed necessary.

In August, Mosley was not present as the crisis unfolded. Pausing only to beg more money from William Morris at Cowley, he headed to the Riviera for his customary lengthy summer break at Antibes. He left Harold Nicolson behind to mind the party shop in his absence. Nicolson had resigned from his diary editor's job on the *Evening Standard* to edit the New Party's weekly newspaper *Action* which was underwritten by Morris with an initial £5,000 and a guarantee of annual payments of £15,000 for the first two years of the paper's life. Spurred on by encouraging missives from Mosley, Nicolson spent more money hiring staff.

Mosley's life on the Riviera as the country collapsed into chaos took on its usual tenor of parties and partner swapping. Among the celebrities holidaying with the Mosleys were the photographer Cecil Beaton, playwright and songwriter Noël Coward, the novelist Michael Arlen, Mosley's former mistress Maxine Elliott and his current flame, Lottsie Fabre-Luce, wife of the head of the French bank Crédit Lyonnais. Once again, a familiar pattern repeated itself. A desperately unhappy Cimmie found herself torn between looking after her children and trying to stop her husband from blatantly making assignations with the petite, blonde and blue-eyed Lottsie. Cimmie succeeded to the extent of conceiving her third child, but events at home soon called Mosley back to Britain.

In mid-August, the Depression arrived in Europe. The collapse of the Austrian bank Kredit Anstalt signalled the breakdown of the international banking system that heralded a crisis of confidence in capitalism itself. On 22 August, the MacDonald government learned that American financiers would not advance loans to bail out Britain unless May's full 20 per cent cut in the dole was implemented.

On 23 August, MacDonald saw the King and offered the government's resignation. But George V had already secured the agreement of Baldwin and the Liberals to serve in a National Government under MacDonald's nominal leadership. MacDonald agreed but unfortunately his party failed to see events in the same light, and with the exception of Philip Snowden, Mosley's old boss J H Thomas and one other minor minister, the entire Cabinet resigned, leaving a tiny 'National Labour' rump around MacDonald to join what was, in all but name, a Conservative government. Lloyd George, Churchill and Mosley were all kept out of the new regime.

The major national crisis that met Mosley on his return from the Riviera was matched by a minor crisis within the New Party. Sellick Davies, the national treasurer, had absconded with the party's funds to a casino in Dieppe in the company of one of its MPs, Robert Forgan, who wrote a letter to Mosley demanding £500, with a veiled threat to resign and expose the party to more scandal should the cash not be forthcoming.

Yet neither the tragedy of national bankruptcy nor the comedy of errant party officials dented Mosley's sublime self-confidence. Meeting him at Dover, Harold Nicolson found Mosley serenely

Harold Nicolson a friend and editor of Mosley's newspaper *Action*

cheerful. While recognising that the crisis he had predicted was now upon them, Mosley was realistic enough to realise that his depleted New Party band was not ready to confront it. Under Nicolson's fastidious editorship the launch of *Action* went ahead with a bizarre mix of Mosley's rhetoric on the front page, and the inside pages dominated by esoteric contributions from Nicolson's intellectual friends – including gardening notes contributed by his wife, Vita Sackville-West.

Mosley continued to wage the political battle: he concluded a swingeing Commons attack on the new National Government by proclaiming that the way out of the crisis was not the *way of the monk but the way of the athlete . . . the simple question before the House is whether Britain is to meet its crisis lying down or standing up.*[76] Days later, in front of a crowd of 20,000 at Glasgow, Mosley derided his erstwhile Labour comrades as *a Salvation Army that took to its heels on the day of judgement.*[77]

Communists in the crowd attempted to attack Mosley with razors and pelted him and his bodyguards with rocks. Mosley took a hit to the head, but was protected from further damage by Peter Howard and Kid Lewis, a Jewish former welterweight boxing champion from the East End. Afterwards, Mosley drew the logical conclusion, telling Nicolson: *This forces us to be fascist . . . we need no longer hesitate to create our trained and disciplined force.*[78] They set to discussing uniforms, with Nicolson suggesting grey flannels and shirts with a marigold buttonhole. A few days later, the government removed Britain from the Gold Standard and the chains of financial orthodoxy, and announced the plans for recovery that Mosley had been urging in vain for so long. It followed up by calling a general election for 27 October.

The election saw a determined Establishment campaign to stifle the New Party and silence Mosley. He was banned from the BBC, and a New Party propaganda film, *Crisis*, was barred from the nation's cinemas. Unsurprisingly, he ended the campaign in a state of nervous exhaustion and near-hysteria.

The election results could hardly have been worse for Mosley. The electorate gave the National Government the 'doctor's mandate' it sought with a thumping majority. The Labour Party was reduced to a rump of 51 seats, and the New Party won none at all. Mosley himself, who had taken a sick and pregnant Cimmie's place as candidate for Stoke, had the hitherto unfamiliar experience of coming bottom of the poll.

The New Party's poll figures nationwide were derisory: standing in the same number of seats (26) as the Communists, it scraped just over 36,000 votes to the Communists' 71,000. Clearly, Mosley's first assault on the old party politics had failed. Within days of the poll, he shut down the New Party's London HQ and sacked all but three of its employees. By the end of the year *Action* had closed, too. The paper, despite Nicolson's efforts in attracting contributions from young leftists such as the writer Christopher Isherwood, and the future Labour firebrand Ian Mikardo, was too elitist and eclectic to attain the mass circulation it needed to survive. With articles praising Soviet communism on the one hand, and garbled frothings from the crime writer Peter Cheyney on the other, *Action* reflected the hopeless confusions of the New Party only too accurately.

In *Action's* last issue, on 31 December 1931, Nicolson ruefully admitted: 'We were too highbrow for the general public and too popular for the highbrow.'[79] Mosley himself sounded a note intended to ring heroically, but which emerged as bathos: *We are Pierced and Broken – we Advance . . . we shall win; or at least we shall return upon our shields.*[80]

Birth of the BUF

The First World War created the social conditions for fascism's rise. This was most evident in the nations which had done worst out of the war – Germany, Italy and central Europe – but also in Britain and France, where the slaughter of the trenches shook trust in democracy and deference to the old order. Millions of war veterans were often bitter, alienated from the civilian world and unable or unwilling to adjust to peacetime.

Mussolini's Italian Fascist Party, founded in 1919, was composed of such ex-combatants: violent, resentful, impatient men eager for action for its own sake. Appropriately for a movement which took its name and its logo from the Roman *Fasces* – a bundle of sticks bound around an axe, symbolising the power and punishment wielded by the state – Mussolini's fascism was a ragbag of often contradictory attitudes and ideas held together as much by the forceful personality of its founder, as any coherent ideology.

Though consciously anti-intellectual, fascism was partly derived from the thought and writings of certain 19th-century thinkers: Count Gobineau, the French apostle of racial difference; Auguste Comte, the founder of positivism; Oswald Spengler, the gloomy German prophet of the decline of the West; Houston Stewart Chamberlain, the renegade Englishman who married into the Wagner family and foretold the rise of an Aryan Messiah; Friedrich Nietzsche's exaltation of the superman and his preaching against 'herd morality'[81]; and, finally, Gabriele d'Annunzio,

Italy's most renowned poet, who provided a living example of an ideal fascist life, comprising romance, cruelty, kitsch barbarism, violent military action and bombastic irrationalism.

The 1917 Bolshevik revolution in Russia lent urgency to fascism's mission. It seemed that all the far right's dark warnings were fulfilled. Blood-thirsty, property-threatening 'Reds', preaching the Jewish message of Marx, had seized control of the world's biggest country and their destructive ideology was running riot through a war-weary Europe. Fascism sprang from the combination of the bitterness of defeat in Germany and Austria and the incompleteness of what d'Annunzio termed Italy's 'mutilated victory'.[82]

Until the Depression, Mosley had shown little interest in fascism. Indeed, his move from idiosyncratic Conservatism to Labour had been accompanied by blood-curdling prophecies that aggressive socialism was the wave of the future. But his rhetoric was always tinged with fascist-style appeals to violence, energy, sacrifice and will. Mosley's record as a self-appointed spokesman of the disillusioned First World War generation, and his impatient, forceful personality fitted him perfectly for a future as a fascist leader. It seemed, therefore, inevitable to him and to the many who watched him, that fascism was his destiny.

After the demise of the New Party, in October 1931, it was another year before Mosley formally introduced the British Union of Fascists (BUF). Major encouragement came in December from Lord Rothermere, owner of the *Daily Mail*, who promised to put the powerful support of his Harmsworth Press behind Mosley if he launched a disciplined fascist movement. Mosley did not take the bait at that stage, partly because of Cimmie's violent disapproval – she threatened to put a notice in *The Times* disassociating herself from his politics if he went fascist – and partly because he was exhausted and, she claimed, 'broke'.[83] (This term was always rela-

Mosley and Cimmie campaigning arm in arm 1930

tive given the wealth of the Mosleys, but it is true that Savehay Farm was temporarily let and the Mosleys moved into a cramped central London flat previously occupied by their chauffeur.)

In late 1931, Mosley occupied himself with fencing – at 35 he was still an Olympic-standard performer with the épée – partying, bickering with the pregnant Cimmie and amusing himself watching mud-wrestling contests at the Gargoyle Club. Behind the scenes, however, he was preparing to descend into the mud-wrestling arena himself. Harold Nicolson wrote a lengthy letter warning Mosley against the step he was about to take. England, he said, was not Italy or Germany. It had no tradition of secret societies or militarism, and any attempt to introduce fascism would fail.

Mosley, however, turned a deaf ear. In January 1932, he left for Rome on the fact-finding visit he had promised to make in the

MUD WRESTLING 69

last edition of *Action*. He met Mussolini – a fellow fencer – who graciously gave permission for him to use the term 'fascist' for the movement he was contemplating.

Back in England, Nicolson was increasingly worried about the fascist road down which Mosley as marching. Ultimately, he bade a sad political farewell from Mosley: 'If Tom would . . . retire into private life for a bit and then emerge fortified and purged – he will still be Prime Minister of England. But if he gets entangled with the boy's brigade he will be edged gradually into becoming a revolutionary, and into that waste land I cannot follow him.'[84] But Mosley's mind was almost made up. In the *Daily Mail*, he penned a paean to fascist Italy and its Duce: *The mind is hard, concentrated – in a word 'Modern'. The great Italian represents the first emergence of the modern man to power.*[85] Mosley was gambling on the Depression producing a social and political breakdown. He was prepared, he told Nicolson, to take the risk of failure and ridicule that his friend predicted *rather than let the active forces in this country fall into other hands.*[86]

Mosley's descent into the world of Britain's far right was the most catastrophic of the many misjudgments of his reckless career. Until as late as mid-1932, he could have pulled back from the brink, and responded to the continuing overtures from Churchill and Lloyd George, who were still eager to take him into an anti-National Government opposition. Mosley, however, was never willing to play second fiddle to anyone, even to such dynamic eminences as the past and future wartime leaders of his country.

Mosley exaggerated the gravity of the economic crisis that would bring Hitler to power in Germany within six months, but which in Britain was already beginning to recede. Yet he underestimated the resilience of the parliamentary system to shocks and its ability to manage change. Eager for action and dazzled by what he had seen in Italy, Mosley rushed towards the precipice. He also overlooked the engrained conservatism of the British public, particularly its antipathy since Cromwell to militarism in politics; marches and uniforms would not go down well at Whitehall or Westminster.

Mosley's defiant rejection of the 'old politics' and his espousal of fascism were the results of his enduring belief in his 'star' and in the effect that his dynamic persona would have on the inert forces of politics and economics. Again and again, he had demonstrated this impulsive conceit: in crossing the floor of the House over Ireland; in joining Labour – and then leaving it; in founding the New Party and winding it up. However, the step he was now about to take would put him irrevocably beyond the British political pale.

On 27 April 1932, two days after Cimmie had given birth to their third child, Michael ('Mickey'), Mosley chaired a meeting of NUPA, the youth wing of the New Party which had survived the demise of its parent party. The theme was 'The blindness of British politics under the Jew money-power' and the speakers were Arnold Leese, leader of the Imperial Fascist League (IFL) and Henry Hamilton Beamish, a former Tory diehard who ran the influential Britons Publishing Society, responsible for disseminating Nesta Webster's writings and much of the far right's most venomous anti-Semitic literature over the next two decades.

Mosley affected a lofty disdain for the IFL, whose membership could be counted in scores rather than the thousands which Leese's 'Fascist Legions' suggested. Mosley called the group: *One of those*

> Nesta Webster (1867–1960) was the daughter of a Barclays Bank director who stumbled on the 'hidden conspiracy' she claimed lay behind modern history. Between the world wars, she produced a vast corpus of works linking together the Jews, Freemasons, Bolsheviks, German militarists, the occult and shady finance in an ongoing plot to undermine Christian civilisation and establish a world government. Her writings were extremely influential among both outright fascists and the reactionary right.

crank little societies . . . mad about the Jews.[87] Yet despite this disdain, he was ready to cross his Rubicon and proudly proclaim himself a fascist.

Mosley spent the summer in one of his usual playgrounds, the Venice Lido, writing *The Greater Britain* which became the manifesto of the movement he was about to launch. The book is a mix of Mosley's familiar diagnoses and nostrums and a rousing call to Britain's youth to shake off *decadence* and the rule of those Mosley contemptuously called *children* and *old women*. He claimed that democracy's political institutions had been outrun by social and technological change, and needed to adapt to the modern age. His solution was to do away with the corrupt rule of the *old parties*[88] and replace it with a fascist corporate state that would abolish the class struggle. (Mosley's railing against *decadence*, had a hypocritical ring, issuing as it did from a louche playboy lolling on the Lido.)

The Greater Britain indignantly anticipated and refuted charges that Mosley was planning to set up a dictatorship. Debate in a future fascist parliament would be free, he insisted, but once decisions had been taken, the Leader and his cohorts would implement them without further discussion. 'Voluntary Discipline' was to be the new slogan, and life would be run by a *dedicated minority in every town and village capable of sustained effort.*[89] To accompany such windy yet sinister rhetoric, Mosley put his new movement into a literal straitjacket, slavishly imitating Mussolini's fascists. This included black shirts modelled by Mosley on fencing jackets, and the Italian fascist axe and canes symbol.

He entered negotiations with Britain's other fading fascist groups to join forces under his leadership in an invigorated new 'Union'. His overtures were largely successful. Neil Francis Hawkins and E Mandeville Roe from the British Fascists, despite the violent disapproval of Rotha Linton-Orman the BF leader herself, brought over the bulk of the BF. Only Arnold Leese's IFL, regarding Mosley as a mere opportunist, held aloof.

On 1 October 1932, Mosley summoned 32 chosen companions to the old HQ of the New Party in London's Great George Street for the ceremonial unfurling of the flag of the BUF. To his assembled followers, Mosley proclaimed: *We ask those who join us to march with us in a great and hazardous adventure. We ask them to be prepared to sacrifice all, but to do so for no small or unworthy ends. We ask them to dedicate their lives to building in this country a movement of the modern age . . . Those who march with us will certainly face abuse, misunderstanding, bitter animosity and possibly the ferocity of struggle and danger. In return we can only offer them the deep belief that they are fighting that a great land may live . . .*[90]

Diana

In his personal and political life, 1932 was the watershed year for Mosley. In the spring, just as he took the decision to make the great leap into fascism, he met the woman who would become his chosen companion on the rocky road of the rest of his life: Diana (Mitford) Guinness.

Mosley and Diana formally met when they were seated together by their hostess at a dinner. He lost no time in charming the young mother of two – telling her that he had noticed her twice before, in Venice, and at a Park Lane party at the home of Sir Philip Sassoon, a wealthy Jewish socialite. Despite, or because of, Mosley's reputation as a sexual and political buccaneer, Diana was smitten. In her autobiography she puts the attraction in political terms, praising Mosley's 'lucid, forceful and persuasive'[91] plans to cure the economic crisis. However, the attraction was sexual, too, and British high society's second-most notorious affair of the 1930s – after that of the Prince of Wales and Mrs Simpson – was instantly underway.

Diana had packed plenty of experience into her 21 years. She was the third daughter of Lord and Lady Redesdale and her family, the Mitfords, were conventional members of Mosley's own social circle. With her wide china blue eyes, perfect complexion and sculpted facial structure, Diana was easily the most beautiful of the six sisters, and soon escaped the tedium of Cotswold country life by marrying Bryan Guinness of the brewing dynasty. In quick

Unity, Diana and Nancy Mitford outside St Margaret's Church Westminster.

succession, she gave birth to two sons, Jonathan and Desmond, and mingled with the likes of Winston Churchill, the Sitwells, and artistic admirers including Evelyn Waugh, Augustus John, Henry Lamb and Carrington and Lytton Strachey of the Bloomsbury set.

Despite her hectic social life and young family, Diana was a stereotypical bored wealthy wife when she met Mosley. Her youthful marriage had already palled, and she was ready, not for idle dalliance, but to be swept off her feet and to defy social etiquette and her family in the process. At first, the affair followed the usual course of Mosley's adulterous amours: engineered encounters at parties; assignations in Mosley's Ebury Street flat; public flirtation and private passion – all conducted within the rules of the game tacitly accepted within their circle, even by their respective spouses.

In June 1932 Diana threw a lavish Thames-side river party to celebrate her 22nd birthday. A belligerent Churchill, inveighing

A NOTORIOUS AFFAIR 75

against Stanley Spencer's art to the horror of his effete former private secretary, Eddie Marsh, and a 'worse for wear' Augustus John were among the guests, as was Mosley. 'I wore a pale grey dress of chiffon and tulle,' Diana recalled, 'and all the diamonds I could lay my hands on. We danced until the day broke, a pink and orange sunrise which gilded the river.'[92]

Against this Noël Cowardish backdrop, Mosley made a passionate declaration of love. He could not leave Cimmie, he said, but subject to that constraint, his life would be dedicated to Diana. She responded in kind – she too was deeply in love and, in contrast to Mosley, was ready to take the socially shocking step of leaving her husband for him. Their life's course was set.

For the moment, however, they made deceitful plans to fool their spouses like any adulterous couple. Mosley arranged for Diana to meet him 'by chance' at Avignon as he drove to Venice where Cimmie, convalescing after the birth of Mickey, and suffering persistent kidney trouble, would join them. Diana, too, fell ill, struck down by diphtheria. Eventually the Mosleys and the Guinnesses got together at Venice in a party that included a trio of young Churchillians – Winston's son, Randolph, and his disciples Brendan Bracken and Bob Boothby.

As had become his holiday habit, Mosley was openly neglectful of Cimmie. Between bouts of working on *The Greater Britain* he took Diana off in a gondola for adulterous afternoons. (The couple's urgent need for each other sometimes burst through the bounds of decent discretion. At dinner one evening, Mosley told Boothby imperiously: *Bob, I shall need your room tonight between midnight and 4am.* Boothby inquired reasonably 'But where shall I sleep?' The answer: *On the beach.* He did.[93])

Cimmie, ill and dumpy after her pregnancy, and 12 years older than Diana, was crushed by Mosley's cruel flaunting of his latest conquest. After their return home, she wrote to him pathetically: 'If you had said you would like to take Diana out for the day

Sunday, I would have known where I was. Oh, darling, darling, don't let it be like that. I will truly understand if you give me a chance. But I am so kept in the dark.' Then, in a flash of repressed rage about the London love nest where her husband and Diana had consummated their passion, she burst out: 'That bloody, damnable, cursed Ebury [Street]. How often does she come there?'

The seriousness of Diana's love for him, and his need for her, was dawning on Mosley. He decided to own up to his past adulteries to his wife. But instead of clearing the air, the confession left Cimmie more crushed than ever. 'But they are all my friends!' she wailed after the long list of names was out. Once more, Boothby was called on – this time to comfort Cimmie. Briefing Boothby, Mosley told him that he had divulged all his adulteries. 'All, Tom?' asked Boothby, aghast. *Yes all – except, of course, for her sister and stepmother.*[94]

While Mosley feverishly prepared for the launch of the BUF and carried on with Diana, Cimmie took her children to the French spa of Contrexville in September to try to regain her health. She and Tom exchanged friendly letters in their customary baby language – full of references to 'porkers' and 'squash-tails'. But beneath the *badinage* Cimmie's deep pain would not go away.

Grief and Guilt

Mosley's commitment to fascism divided his family and friends. Cimmie, despite her earlier threats to dissociate herself from his new enthusiasm, remained loyal – even working on designs for a fascist flag. Mosley's mother, Lady Maud, eagerly signed up to her man-child's new cause, and there was a plan for Osbert Sitwell to write a fascist anthem set to a military march by Sousa. Many of Mosley's circle, however, shared Harold Nicolson's pained distaste for 'Bermondsey boys with *gummiknupfel* [rubber truncheons]'[95], and fought shy of fascism.

Mosley positively flaunted those aspects of his movement that most repelled his critics. On 15 October 1932, a fortnight after the BUF was launched, he tested the waters by holding the first of countless BUF public meetings – in Trafalgar Square. Cimmie and his children were on hand to watch Mosley, flanked by eight muscular young men in black shirts and grey trousers, sporting Union flags and the fascist logo, preach his message. Also there were his past and present lovers, Georgia Sitwell and Diana Guinness.

A week later, at the Farringdon Memorial Hall where both the Labour and New Parties had been launched, Mosley held a second meeting. Heckled, he was unwise enough to let a hostile question from a Jewish journalist provoke him into an anti-Semitic sneer about *class warriors from Jerusalem*, admitting that fascists were hostile to those Jews who were *anti-British*[96] or who financed Communism.

There was no shortage of cautionary counselling from friends such as Bob Boothby and Harold Nicolson, but Mosley chose to ignore it. What's more, he was already paying a high price for surrendering to thuggish anti-Semitism. The Jewish industrialist, Israel Sieff, of Marks and Spencer, heading an association of 50 business leaders worried by the Depression, had approached Irene offering to finance Mosley. Now the spectacle of fascism in ugly action had its predictable consequences. On 31 October, Irene met Sieff again: 'After [Mosley's] inane jibe to the heckler as coming from Jerusalem, Sieff told me he was now so bitter he will not give him money . . . oh, how tactless Tom is! It makes me sick.'[97]

In 1932, the Democrat Franklin Delano Roosevelt (1882–1945) became President as head of a coalition of leftist idealists, poor Southerners and ethnic minorities. He launched the New Deal, a Keynesian programme that called for public funding to combat economic depression. A ruthless pragmatist, he kept the US out of the war as long as he could, and died, exhausted, a week before Hitler.

Cimmie's other sister, Baba Metcalfe, was less critical of Mosley. She enthusiastically endorsed fascism, becoming known to wags as 'Baba Blackshirt'. Baba's fascist stance was doubtless reinforced by the fact that Mosley was cuckolding her hapless husband 'Fruity' in a parallel affair to his liaison with Diana.

Mosley had not yet cut all his ties to respectability and the establishment. In the winter of 1932–3, he again hob-nobbed with Churchill and Lloyd George. He politely, and often brilliantly, debated fascism in public: with Lloyd George's politician daughter Megan on the BBC; with Clement Attlee at the Cambridge Union; and against the Independent Labour Party's Jimmy Maxton at the Friends' Meeting House on Euston Road, with Lloyd George in the chair.

The election of F D Roosevelt in November 1932 as US President was bad news for Mosley's main remaining political card – his gamble that the Western world would be plunged into a crisis so cataclysmic that only fascism would save it. Roosevelt's New Deal slowly began to turn the US economy – and in its wake the world – around.

It would be left to another charismatic politician, one with a darker agenda than Roosevelt's, who also came to power in January 1933, to create the political maelstrom that would finally beckon Mosley before blowing him into oblivion: Adolf Hitler.

In April 1933, Mosley and Cimmie travelled to Rome. Mosley appeared alongside the Duce on the balcony of his residence on the Palazzo Venezia, and, with a group of British Blackshirts, witnessed a Fascist march-past. When they returned to London it was clear that Cimmie had not shaken off her physical illness or her emotional malaise. 'I have been fearfully unhappy,'[98] she told a friend. She complained of persistent back pains and agonising abdominal cramps. Her doctor diagnosed a grumbling appendix. After dropping Nicholas off at prep school, Cimmie returned to Denham for a final row with Mosley over Diana. He left for his new mistress, leaving Cimmie to write a last letter of regret and reproach in their nursery language.

The following day, 9 May 1933, Cimmie's pain grew unendurable. She was rushed to the London Clinic to remove her by now perforated appendix. The operation seemed to go well, and Mosley left her bedside for dinner with Diana – who had meanwhile divorced Bryan and was living alone in Eaton Square – and her sister Unity.

Lady Irene Curzon in 1928. Her support and affection towards her brother-in-law, Mosley, was to end in estrangement and litigation

At first, Cimmie appeared to rally. But a post-operative infection set in which turned to peritonitis. In the pre-antibiotics age there was little that medicine could do to save her but, as the doctors told her family, she did not seem to want to save herself. Cimmie knew, her sisters felt, that she had finally lost the battle for Mosley to Diana, who the Curzon sisters bitterly held responsible for Cimmie's failure to resist her illness. Irene flew home from holidaying in Italy to join Mosley, his mother and Baba in a week-long deathbed vigil. Mosley, stricken with guilt and grief, rarely left his dying wife.

On the morning of 16 May, Cimmie murmured to Mosley, 'I am going. Goodbye, my Buffy,'[99] and slipped into a coma which lasted through an intolerably long afternoon. Mosley remained by her bedside, distractedly muttering words of love to the unconscious woman. Cimmie died early that evening.

Mosley was genuinely shattered by his wife's death. Her body lay in the chapel at Cliveden while a pink sarcophagus, designed by the doyen of British architects, Sir Edwin Lutyens, was sunk into the garden at Denham. A year later, in May 1934, her body was transferred there. Mosley inscribed the tomb with the words:

MY BELOVED. After he finally left Denham, the sarcophagus was damaged by grave robbers who believed rumours that Cimmie had been buried with her jewellery. Her body was moved again to its final resting place in Denham church.

Building the Blackshirts

For all his grief, it was not in Mosley's nature to mourn for long, and within days of Cimmie's death he had resumed his affairs with Diana and Baba.

Mosley's principal means of shaking off his despair, however, was political action. He plunged into building the BUF: recruiting; holding public meetings and marches; drumming up publicity. His mother took Cimmie's place as the first lady of British fascism; Diana was to be kept under wraps for years.

Mosley brooked no opposition to his domination of the movement. Imitating Hitler and Mussolini, he insisted on being referred to as 'The Leader', adopted the stiff-armed fascist salute and the greeting 'Hail Mosley!' Although authoritarianism was part and parcel of fascist theory and practice, Mosley seemed to lose all touch with the parochial realities of British politics in giving the BUF such an unashamedly paramilitary style. This, together with the violence associated with the movement from its earliest days – meted out to rival fascists who refused to enrol under Mosley's banner, as well as to its enemies on the left – repelled many. Nevertheless, the BUF enrolled members across Britain.

From the New Party came Robert Forgan, Mosley's erratic deputy, and W E D Allen, who would continue his role as an MI5 mole inside the new movement. From Rotha Linton-Orman's BF, bringing with him its membership list, came Neil Francis Hawkins, an enthusiast for uniforms who became the BUF's

William Joyce

national organiser. Ian Hope Dundas was another military martinet who would play an important role in cementing the BUF's links – not least its secret financial subsidies – with fellow fascists in Europe. Alexander Raven Thomson was the self-styled intellectual of Mosley's movement, responsible for a book on the corporate state as well as turgid articles expounding fascist theory in BUF journals. A K Chesterton, a cousin of G K Chesterton, was also a writer, but of a more combative, polemical type. Soon after the founding of the BUF, he penned the first official hagiography of its chief: *Mosley: Portrait of a Leader*.

Mosley's most notorious recruit was William Joyce. Joyce was an American-born, Irish-raised extreme British patriot and Mosley's equal as a rabble-rousing orator. Disfigured by a scar across his cheek inflicted by a razor-wielding Communist in the 1920s, Joyce was a fanatical fascist whose notoriety as the wartime radio traitor 'Lord Haw-Haw' would make him the most reviled man in England.

One of the rare recruits who joined the BUF from the left was John Beckett, another brilliant demagogue. A former secretary to Clement Attlee, Beckett had become an Independent Labour Party MP. Beckett's Westminster years had ended when he snatched the Mace of the House of Commons and ran out of the chamber in a typically theatrical protest against unemployment. Labour's staid leadership was horrified, and Beckett was frozen out and into Mosley's waiting arms. Warm-hearted, impulsive and extreme, Beckett's hatred for his former Labour comrades was as strong as his inability to accept the disciplines of fascism or Mosley's leadership.

In June 1933, a month after Cimmie's death, Mosley felt strong enough to organise a march on London's streets by 1,000 Blackshirts. The rest of the summer was spent mainly in Europe, as Mosley pursued his relationship with a besotted Baba. He spent some time with his children at Denham, and in frequent lone visits to the Cliveden chapel where he communed with Cimmie's spirit. He even consulted a medium in an effort to contact Cimmie in the hereafter.

In September 1933, the BUF leased Whitelands, a former Teachers' Training College on Battersea Park Road, Chelsea, turning it into a fortress HQ named 'The Black House' in imitation of Hitler's 'Brown House' in Munich. Mosley and the other leaders had their offices here, guarded by up to 200 uniformed Blackshirts who lived in dormitories under military discipline, parading to bugle calls, drilling and practising boxing, athletics and martial arts. This elite squad would travel in armour-plated vans to protect Mosley and other fascist speakers at their rowdy public meetings.

Mosley was building his movement, appointing regional organisers, recognising local branches, appealing both to the middle classes and the unemployed in the towns, and to farmers and agricultural labourers in the depressed countryside. Still, the profile of the party was patchy. It was strong in London's East End, where there was a traditional hostility to immigration and a high incidence of Jewish settlement – then estimated at 150,000. Other BUF bulwarks were coastal resorts, particularly in Sussex, slump-hit South Wales, Mosley's old political heartland in Birmingham and the depressed cities of the north, especially Leeds, Liverpool and Manchester. It was at a meeting at Manchester's Free Trade Hall in mid-October that Mosley tried out the Hitler-style tactics of deliberately arriving late to build audience anticipation, marching down a central aisle flanked by flag-bearing Blackshirts, and speaking from a high rostrum illuminated by searchlights.

BUF membership grew rapidly, reaching around 15,000 by the end of 1933. It was mainly young, middle class and male, but not overwhelmingly so. Attracted by 'modern' fascist policies, such as ending the widespread practice of sacking women from their jobs on marriage, many women joined the Blackshirts – particularly in depressed Lancashire. Eventually women, under the titular leadership of 'Ma Mosley' – Lady Maud, ably seconded by an ex-suffragette, Mary Richardson – constituted one-quarter of the BUF's membership, and Mosley himself later acknowledged the part they played: *My movement has been largely built up by the fanaticism of women; they hold ideas with tremendous passion. Without the women I could not have got one-quarter of the way.*[100]

For some women, and many men, the Blackshirts became not just a political party but an all-encompassing way of life. Whole families joined, taking part in regular BUF social events and even

Mosley reviewing women members of the British Union of Fascists

holidaying each summer at a Blackshirt camp at Selsey on the Sussex coast. There were even Blackshirt weddings and funerals.

Mosley sought to increase influence and support for his movement beyond the membership by imitating Communist tactics of forming 'front' organisations: groups of fascist-sympathising fellow-travellers. One such was the January Club, a dining group of socially prominent people who broke bread with prominent fascist speakers. January Club guests included: Major Francis Yeats-Brown, author of the bestsellers *Lives of a Bengal Lancer* and *Winged Victory*; Brigadier-General Sir Edward Spears, a close friend of Churchill's; the colonial administrator Lord Lloyd, another of Churchill's friends; the military theorist Basil Liddell Hart; aristocrats such as Lord Middleton and the Earl of Iddesleigh; the jurist Lord Russell of Liverpool; the literary journalists Sir John Squire and Philip Magnus; and the historian Sir Charles Petrie. Similar front groups were established in the army, the civil service, the universities and even in the public schools, including Mosley's alma mater, Winchester.

There was a strong bias towards the military and the empire in the BUF's leadership. Its middle ranks were filled with retired colonels and majors and former Imperial district officers. A modern profession which seemed inordinately attracted to Mosley's fascism, with its love of sport, were the 'speed kings' so prominent in the record-smashing inter-war years. The holder of the world land speed racing record, Sir Malcolm Campbell, sported fascist colours on his car 'Bluebird', and other racing adherents included Vernon Pickering and the lady dirt-track driver 'Fabulous' Fay Taylour. The first Englishman to fly, subsequently the successful manufacturer of the Avro aircraft, Sir Alliott Verdon Roe, was also a supporter; while the flying magazine, *The Aeroplane* was a virtual house journal of fascism under its editor C J Grey and his deputy Geoffrey Dorman, a former comrade of Mosley in the RFC.

The novelist Henry Williamson, author of *Tarka the Otter*, whose fascism was fuelled by his war-time experiences and his painful knowledge of the disastrous slump in rural England, joined the BUF and became a slavish admirer of Mosley, whom he put into his naïve novels as 'Sir Hereward Birkin'. Another former military man who turned to writing when the army rejected his advanced ideas for the mechanisation of warfare was Major-General J F C 'Boney' Fuller, a father of the tank.

Despite the sympathy of these celebrities, most of the political establishment steered well clear of Mosley in his new colours. As with Churchill and Lloyd George, distrust of this maverick was now endemic in the political class, who shared Stanley Baldwin's belief that Mosley was 'a cad and a wrong 'un'.[101]

In January 1934, after visiting Mussolini in Rome and being urged by the Duce to back Mosley, Lord Rothermere swung the might of the Harmsworth Press behind the BUF. The *Daily Mail* carried an editorial written by Rothermere himself under the banner headline 'Hurrah for the Blackshirts!', while the *Mail*'s sister paper the *Sunday Dispatch* reported the adhesion of a debutante to the movement under the heading 'Beauty Joins the Blackshirts' and offered a £5 prize for a photo of 'Britain's most beautiful Blackshirt'. Meanwhile the *Evening Standard* ran a competition for readers to sum up 'Why I like the Blackshirts'[102] on a postcard. With this support, BUF membership shot up, reaching an estimated 50,000 by mid-1934. All augured well for the future of British fascism, but the first flush of Mosley's success was not to last.

Olympia

Founding and building the BUF had taken its toll on Mosley's precarious health, and that winter he succumbed to one of his regular complaints, phlebitis a potentially fatal inflammation of the veins in his legs. Leaving his children at Denham with their Aunt Irene, and with Baba distracted by her new affair with the Italian ambassador, Count Dino Grandi, he travelled to Provence with Diana to recuperate.

By April 1934, he was ready to return to the fray, and the BUF staged its largest meeting to date and the first of its monster indoor rallies, at the Royal Albert Hall, where 10,000 filled the venue. An orchestra played the Nazi anthem the *Horst Wessel Lied* and the Italian fascist hymn *Giovinezza*. As the leader entered with his party flag, the audience rose to sing a paean composed for the occasion: 'Mosley, leader of thousands! / Hope of our manhood, we proudly hail thee! / Raise we this song of allegiance / For we are sworn and shall not fail thee.'[103]

Mosley launched into a call for action and sacrifice, described by his son Nicholas: 'My father's voice comes out lashing like some great sea: it is pulverising; it is also, from a human being, like something carried far away beyond sense. It sends shivers up and down the spine – of both wonder and alarm – what is it all for, this yell for immolation? People at the end of such a speech . . . were on their feet and cheering: it was as if they had been lifted high on a wave; what did it matter if they were hurled against, or over, the top of, a cliff?'

Mosley addressing a packed Albert Hall

Mosley's insistence on adopting the trappings of Italian fascism, and, increasingly, German Nazism, was alienating many, as the liberal journalist Ivor Brown noted: 'These devotees of democracy insist on wearing the uniform, using the salute and generally practising the rigmarole of the Italian Fascists . . . [if they] insist on aping the Italian model in its choice of shirtings and salaams, they can hardly expect the public to disassociate them entirely from its practice and philosophy.'[104]

In fact, there was a widening contradiction between the BUF's proudly proclaimed patriotism and its mimicking of foreign forms. Like the British Communist Party, it was widely perceived to be an alien implant in the British body politic.

In June 1934, came the watershed for British fascism. Mosley determined to build on the success of the Albert Hall rally by staging an even larger meeting in London's then biggest venue: the Olympia stadium in Kensington. This time the left was determined not to let Mosley pass without a struggle. The Communist Party rallied its militants to halt British fascism in its tracks. As a popular chant of the left had it: 'Hitler and Mosley, what are they for? Thuggery, buggery, hunger and war!'

The Communist Party paper, the *Daily Worker*, co-ordinated five columns to converge on Olympia, where an audience of 12,000 was to hear Mosley, protected by 2,000 Blackshirts. But if the Communists were determined to disrupt his meeting, Mosley was equally set on appealing to opinion formers beyond. Invitations to Olympia had been issued to MPs and members of the left-liberal intelligentsia including the writers Aldous Huxley, Naomi Mitchison, Storm Jameson, Vera Brittain and the scientist Ritchie Calder.

Those arriving at Olympia had to fight their way through a crowd of some 3,000 chanting anti-fascists outside, and the meeting began an hour late. The anti-fascists had infiltrated the meeting itself as the BUF had given away at least 2,000 tickets, many of which had been acquired by Communists who were seated in groups throughout the hall.

As soon as Mosley started to speak, the heckling began, with groups or individual interrupters shouting 'Fascism means murder!' and 'Down with Mosley!' The chanting drowned out even the amplified voice of the Leader, and he halted, hands on hips, while Blackshirt stewards attempted to evict the hecklers. Fights broke out in the audience as the stewards struggled through the seats to reach their tormentors. Neil Francis Hawkins even pursued one of them on to the girders supporting the stadium's roof, while spotlights played dramatically across the hall.

The Communist wrecking tactics worked well. As soon as the stewards had ejected one group of hecklers, another would start up. The fascists responded with rough treatment once they had manhandled the interrupters into the corridors outside. Here too, there were witnesses. One, Geoffrey Lloyd MP, stated: 'Again and again as five or six fascists carried out an interrupter by arms and legs, several other fascists were engaged in hitting or kicking his helpless body.'[105]

Three shocked Tory MPs, W J Anstruther-Grey, J Scrymgeour-Wedderburn and T J O'Connor, hurried to the offices of *The Times* to write a letter of protest in time for the next day's paper: 'We were involuntary witnesses of wholly unnecessary violence inflicted by uniformed Blackshirts on interrupters. Men and women were knocked down and were still assaulted and kicked on the floor. It will be a matter of surprise to us if there were no fatal injuries.'[106]

In fact, the violence produced no lasting injuries. Many people were treated for cuts and bruises, but only three – one anti-fascist and two Blackshirts – were hurt seriously enough to be detained in hospital overnight. The real damage inflicted at Olympia was to the reputation of Mosley's movement, which became indelibly tarred with the brush of violence and thuggery. Mosley held a press conference the following day at which he produced an array of weapons – knuckledusters, knives and coshes – which he claimed his stewards had confiscated from their opponents, but the damage had been done.

Not all the publicity was unfavourable to the Blackshirts, however. In reply to his Conservative colleagues who had protested in *The Times*, M W Beaumont MP wrote to the paper complaining that as the police had made no effort to keep order inside the hall (in fact, they had been asked to stay away by Mosley) the use of violence by the Blackshirts was 'the only way in which those putting forward an unknown and controversial case can obtain a hearing'.[107]

Mosley's case was summed up by an elder statesman who had always admired him, Lloyd George, who wrote in the *Sunday Pictorial*: 'It is difficult to explain why the fury of the champions of free speech should be concerned so exclusively . . . not on those who attempted to prevent the expression of feelings of which they disapproved, but against those who fought, however roughly, for freedom of speech.'[108]

Protecting the fascists' freedom of speech had become Mosley's justification for his strong-arm tactics against the real threat of organised violence from the left. However, he could not disguise his enthusiasm for fascism's young bloods, nor did he honestly confront the contradiction that fascism in power would crush the freedom of speech of its critics and opponents.

Privately, Lloyd George wrote nostalgically to Mosley: 'You are having a very exciting time and I envy you your experience. At your age I went through a period of riot and tumult in my endeavour to convey my ideas to a resentful public.'[109] Welcome as such support was from the former Prime Minister, Mosley knew that the Communists had won the battle for public opinion over Olympia.

It was the violence of such meetings, and rumours of rough justice administered to errant Blackshirts in 'punishment cellars' at the Black House, which first seems to have drawn the serious attention of the secret services to Mosley's movement. In November 1933, a meeting was convened at the Home Office to discuss the BUF. Representatives of the Metropolitan Police, Special Branch and MI5 decided to start systematically collecting intelligence on the fascists and monitoring the threat they posed to public order and democracy.

The violent episodes at Olympia profoundly shocked the British public. Forgetting that such political violence had been commonplace in the 18th and 19th centuries, many felt that the scenes at Olympia had been 'un-British', and the government drew up secret plans to clamp down on the BUF.

Yet the most important consequence of Olympia for Mosley was the withdrawal of the support of Lord Rothermere's press empire, only six months after he had put its weight behind the Blackshirts. It was widely believed – not least by Mosley himself – that a consortium of Jewish businessmen had threatened

Rothermere with withdrawing their advertising from his papers unless he dropped Mosley. In July 1934, Rothermere summoned Mosley and broke the news. Immediately, Mosley went public in the BUF's house journal *The Blackshirt*, accusing the press baron of being a Conservative rather than a genuine fascist. Mosley also wrote: *We no longer admit Jews to membership of our movement because (a) they have bitterly attacked us and (b) they have organised as an international movement setting their racial interests above the national interests and are, therefore, unacceptable as members of a national movement which aims at national organisation and revival.*[110] Mosley concluded by alleging that the majority of attacks on fascists were carried out by Jews.

Responding, Rothermere listed the unacceptable faces of fascism: the term itself, the BUF's aim of setting up a dictatorship to replace parliamentary democracy, and its increasing anti-Semitism. The list raises the question as to why Rothermere had supported the Blackshirts in the first place, other than as a ginger group to tweak the Tory Party's tail. But for Mosley, there was no turning back. He had nailed his colours too firmly to the fascist mast.

Financing Fascism

For decades, how Mosley funded the BUF remained a mystery. The New Party had collapsed into bankruptcy, and Mosley himself had felt the pinch. Yet within months he had launched a new national movement, staged expensive mass rallies and produced three journals (*The Blackshirt*, the more intellectual *Fascist Quarterly* and a revived *Action*) not to mention supporting a large London HQ with scores of salaried staff and its permanent Blackshirt Defence Squad (a direct translation of the German *Schutzstaffel*, the SS).

Mosley always hotly denied that his 'patriotic' movement depended on foreign finance in the way that Britain's Communists were propped up by Stalin's 'Moscow gold'. Apart from his own funds and generous donations from rich benefactors, he said the movement generated its own income. Local branches financed themselves from events such as sales, socials, dances, auctions and appeals. Individual members paid monthly subscriptions (a shilling if employed; fourpence if jobless) and saved to buy their black shirts for seven shillings and sixpence, a transaction on which the BUF turned a modest profit. Nevertheless, this did not explain the source of all the money that bankrolled the BUF.

Shortly after Mosley's death, letters to Count Dino Grandi, Baba's lover and the Italian ambassador in London, were uncovered containing positive proof of Mussolini's regular subventions to Mosley. The money was channelled through emissaries and laundered via various currencies – sterling, US dollars, German marks and French and Swiss francs – confirming stories from disaffected fascists that they had seen BUF officials rushing around the Black House clutching bundles of foreign banknotes. The details had apparently been arranged during Mosley's second trip to Italy, and the cash had started to flow in mid-1933. Mosley himself, reported Grandi, had personally collected a lump sum of £20,000 from the embassy in a sealed package, and had expressed his gratitude for the Duce's generosity.

MI5 was aware of the payments through its agents, including W E D 'Bill' Allen. Allen, who retained a genuine loyalty to Mosley despite his work for MI5, used the bank accounts of his printing business to filter some of Mussolini's money into Britain from Swiss sources. Another conduit for funds was Ian Hope Dundas, Mosley's chief of staff. He made frequent visits to Italy, picking up packets of cash in different denominations at various locations. A third BUF chief who was aware of the payments was F M Box, a former Tory Party bureaucrat and the aptly-named box-wallah office manager of the party.

The money paid by the Italians to the BUF totalled between £36,000 and £60,000 a year – a large sum in the 1930s, amounting to well over £1 million in today's values. In 1936, however, following a catastrophic decline in BUF membership, the Italians slashed their funding to just £1,000 a month, prompting a purge of BUF staff in which half of its salaried HQ officials, and all its paid speakers – including William Joyce – and most of its regional organisers were sacked. In March 1937, the Italian subventions ceased altogether after the BUF failed to make progress in London local elections. Further cuts in 1938 and 1939 reduced the BUF's annual outgoings to £13,000. The numbers on its payroll fell from 350 in 1936 to less than 50 in 1939.

Mosley himself was the BUF's chief cash cow after Mussolini. Over its lifetime, he contributed an estimated £100,000 to his movement. The published accounts of the BUF show a small deficit in its opening year, and surpluses in the two subsequent years. Together, the subscriptions and donations totalled nearly £37,000 in the first year, more than £75,000 in the second and over £84,000 in the third before dropping again to £34,000 in 1938–40, of which no less than £24,000 came from Mosley himself.

As in Germany, Italy and France, businessmen and industrialists were another major source of funds. In his New Party days, besides the £50,000 he had received from the motor manufacturer Sir William Morris, Mosley had obtained £5,000 each from Lord Portal and the tobacco magnate Cunliffe Owen. Donors to the BUF included the shipping tycoon Lord Inchape, the aircraft manufacturer Sir A V Roe, Baron Tollemache, Lord Lloyd, the Earl of Glasgow, Sir Charles Petrie and Alex Scrimgeour, a rich stockbroker who gave the movement more than £11,000, but

Early but brief supporters of Mosley's BUF were the press barons Harmsworth, Lord Rothermere and Lord Northcliffe

BUSINESS SUPPORT 97

who transferred his largesse to William Joyce's Nazi splinter group when Joyce left the BUF. There was also some financial support from textile firms, such as Courtaulds, who were under threat from foreign competition.

A quixotic sideline to Rothermere's backing of the BUF was the press magnate's bid to market a brand of 'Blackshirt' cigarettes. Mosley set up a cover company, New Epoch Products Ltd and a factory was registered to make the cigarettes. Besides Mosley and Ian Hope Dundas, New Epoch's directors included two of the *Daily Mail*'s top journalists: air correspondent Max Pemberton and foreign correspondent G Ward Price, best known for his fawning interviews with Hitler. The company was launched with a starting capital of £12,500 before Rothermere aborted the project in 1934.

Another important media backer of Mosley was Lady Lucy Houston, owner of the magazine *Time & Tide*, who held firmly patriotic views. She gave Mosley £200,000 in 1934 (although her largesse dried up after she read some unflattering remarks about herself in *The Blackshirt*).

After the collapse of the cigarette-manufacturing scheme, Mosley tried to make commercial radio the mainstay of his movement's income. He had studied the growth of radio in the US and estimated that a fascist radio station could make some £5 million a year. Radio would also be a powerful propaganda weapon with which he could circumvent the unofficial ban on himself and his movement imposed by the BBC. (After the Olympia rally, Mosley was banned from the Corporation's airwaves for 20 years.)

Given the BBC's broadcasting monopoly in Britain, the only feasible way of exploiting the radio market was to buy stakes in foreign radio stations that could be heard in Britain, or to set up powerful radio transmitters abroad. Mosley pursued both options. He investigated taking a stake in Radio Normandie in France, a station that could be heard across the Channel. He also bought stakes for future radio franchise licences in Ireland, Belgium and Denmark, and persuaded the Dame of Sark, the autocratic hereditary ruler of one of the Channel Islands, to let him buy a 90 per cent stake in the island's radio concession. But perhaps the biggest coup in his radio campaign was when Diana persuaded Hitler to let Mosley use a transmitter in Germany to beam broadcasts to Britain.

Still, this and Mosley's other radio projects, were aborted by the outbreak of war in 1939. Mosley's belief in radio propaganda would be proved during the war itself, ironically not least by the activities of his erstwhile lieutenant, William Joyce.

As Italian financial support declined, Mosley increasingly looked to Germany to replace it. In this he was moved not only by Germany's ever more prominent role on the international stage, but also by his own movement's rapid adoption of an explicitly anti-Semitic, pro-Nazi style. His main emissary in Germany was the woman who would become his second wife, Diana Guinness.

Diana Guinness

The German Connection – Mosley and Anti-Semitism

For a declared fascist, Mosley had been slow to fully adopt one of the creed's central tenets: anti-Semitism.

So scornful were some of Mosley's fascist rivals about what they saw as his lukewarm adoption of their anti-Semitic doctrines that Arnold Leese, whose Imperial Fascist League had always had an explicitly Nazi orientation – their logo was a swastika on a Union flag – sneered at Mosley as a 'kosher fascist'[111] and accused Cimmie of being Jewish via her maternal American forebears, the Leiters.

> 'The Protocols of the Elders of Zion' was an anti-Semitic work forged by the Okhrana, the Imperial Russian secret police. A document alleged to be the minutes of a 19th century meeting in Prague to plot a long-term Jewish takeover of the world, the 'Protocols' were disseminated in the wake of the 1917 Bolshevik revolution and found a ready audience in Europe. Although widely discredited, they are still commonly available in the Arab world.

Leese's IFL was one of several similar groups whose chief component was anti-Semitism, including the Nordic League, the English Mystery, the English Array and the Britons Society. The influence on British society wielded by the explicitly anti-Semitic groups was limited; their combined membership rarely rose above a few hundred, and their meetings were attended by a handful.

Nonetheless, some of Britain's most virulent anti-Semites –

such as William Joyce and A K Chesterton – joined the BUF and influenced its policy in an anti-Semitic direction. The crisis in the BUF's fortunes after Olympia gave them their opportunity. Chesterton was commissioned by Mosley to write a report on Jewish influence in Britain. Its findings informed Mosley's statement to Rothermere that most assaults carried out on his members were by Jews. (Mosley's bitterness against Jewish influence in Britain was heightened by the fact that it was a group of Jewish businessmen who had reportedly persuaded Rothermere to drop his backing for the BUF.)

Even in the 1930s, when open expressions of racial prejudice were commonplace compared to today, naked anti-Semitism was not a doctrine that could be held by a respectable political party. Expressions of anti-Semitism even within the BUF, therefore, tended to be coded and – albeit lightly – disguised. Jews were often called 'aliens' and 'sons and daughters of Jerusalem'. Occasionally, however, more virulent references, such as comparing Jews to 'cancers' and 'maggots' crept out.

Mosley's move towards gutter politics finally destroyed whatever chances he had of achieving power through conventional electoral means and converted the BUF from a mass into a fringe movement, shouting noisily from the sidelines. As far as the political establishment and the middle classes were concerned, fascism meant thuggery, scuffles on the streets, screaming slogans, 'alien' uniforms and incomprehensible racial obsessions. The gradual recovery of the economy from the mid-1930s, at least in London and the south, increased Mosley's marginalisation, and confirmed his status as a political pariah. What's more, for Mosley, his exclusion from the BBC's airwaves, and his freezing out by former friends at the heart of politics, made him only too receptive to the whispers of his anti-Semitic colleagues who told him that it was all a Jewish plot.

In October 1934, the BUF held another rally in the Albert Hall

BUF rally in Hyde Park 1934

at which Mosley made his anti-Semitism explicit. His enemies, he declared, were both the long-established 'big Jews' in business, seen as a threat to the national economy; and the more recently arrived 'little Jews' who gathered in ghetto-like communities in the East End, swamping the indigenous British identity of their hosts.

At the same time, the BUF was being driven into its own ghettos. From its peak in mid-1934, it began to haemorrhage both members and support after Olympia, the withdrawal of the backing of the Rothermere press, and its increasing identification with violence, anti-Semitism and the generally unpopular Nazism of Hitler's Germany.

In response, Mosley concentrated his resources on his heartland areas of bedrock support – principally the East End – and in populist local campaigns, rather than in attempting a broad national appeal. So weak was his national organisation by the time of the 1935 general election – which returned another landslide National Government majority, and a limited recovery by Labour – that he instructed the BUF to boycott the polls, with the feeble slogan 'Fascism next time'. In 1935, William Joyce campaigned to build the BUF's support in the East End, training local speakers to harp on the themes of Jewish immigration from Nazi Germany and the threat it posed to the native British community.

In its emphasis on immigration, the BUF was becoming a one-song band. Gradual economic recovery and the evident electoral support for the National Government had removed its chief claim to significance: Mosley's belief that the party system had broken down and that parliament and democracy itself needed renewal or outright abolition.

Desperately, the movement cast around for new causes to shore up its flagging support. In 1936, partly in gratitude to its Italian paymasters, it agitated against the League of Nations' weak campaign to oppose Italy's invasion of Abyssinia (Ethiopia) with an economic and diplomatic boycott. The BUF, under the slogan 'Mind Britain's Business', argued that Britain should steer clear of foreign entanglements. The same isolationist arguments were used to oppose intervention in the Spanish Civil War, which broke out in July 1936, in which Hitler and Mussolini poured in aircraft, men and munitions to help General Franco's pro-fascist military rebellion against the left-wing Spanish Republic. But foreign affairs only interested a minority in Britain, and carried little resonance among the working classes whom the BUF were now trying to recruit.

BUF campaigns to encourage protectionism in defence of farmers, and to back tenants' rent strikes against Jewish landlords in the East End, were localised and limited in their effects. Not until the growing threat of war with Germany in the late 1930s did the BUF find a cause – pacifism – which drew a wider public response and an echo of its message to keep out of a 'Jews' war'. In the meantime, its membership plummeted from its peak of around 50,000 in mid-1934 towards the derisory figure of 5,000 in 1936–7.

Meanwhile, Diana Guinness, with great calculation, was plotting her future with Mosley. She had not yet won the status of *maîtresse en titre* to the Leader – Baba Metcalfe was still on the scene, and Diana had to share her 1934 summer holidays with Mosley in the south of France with her rival. There was also a mysterious liaison between Mosley and a film actress, Mary Russell Tavener, whom he had met on a movie set a month after Cimmie's death while planning a BUF propaganda film.

In the late summer of 1934, therefore, possibly with the intention of making Mosley miss her, and perhaps because she believed that an increasingly powerful Reich would be an important source of support for both her beloved and the BUF, Diana accompanied her Hitler-besotted sister Unity to Germany to attend that year's Nuremberg party rally, immortalised in Leni Riefenstahl's *Triumph of the Will*. Diana had prepared for the trip by taking German lessons at the Berlitz School in London.

Unity's chief contact in Hitler's hierarchy, 'Putzi' Hanfstängel, had had second thoughts about her enthusiasm for the Führer. He knew that such marks of sophistication as their heavy make-up would offend Hitler's notions of pure Aryan womanhood. But despite Putzi's discouragement, the two sisters went to a Nuremberg packed with some 700,000 Hitler enthusiasts, and returned with Nazi stars in their eyes. They were not alone in their adulation, for despite the recent bloodshed of the Night of Long Knives, when Hitler launched a purge of his rivals and opponents, several other British visitors – including Diana's rival Baba – travelled to Bavaria for the Nuremberg experience.

Diana spent that winter with Unity in Munich, continuing her German language lessons. After leaving, in early February 1935, she was summoned back. Unity, beside herself with excitement, reported that her months of stalking Hitler had paid off. Her habit of eating at the Osteria Bavaria had finally been rewarded when she had been summoned to Hitler's table and had held a half-hour conversation with the Führer, which had concluded with them agreeing that Germany and Britain should never fight against each other in another war fomented by the Jews.

Leni Riefenstahl (1902–2003) was a cinematic genius and the Hitler's favourite filmmaker. Under lavish Nazi patronage, she produced her twin masterpieces of cinematic propaganda: *Triumph of the Will* (1934) a powerful record of the 1934 Nuremberg rally; and a film on the 1936 Berlin Olympics. Despite her later denials of party membership or sympathy, Riefenstahl was tainted to the end of her long life by her youthful Nazi indiscretion and her films remain monuments of cinematic fascist aesthetics.

Having wormed her way into Hitler's entourage, Unity lost no time in introducing her family and friends to the Führer, turning her Germanophobe parents and brother Tom into fervent fascists in the process.

A month after Unity's first encounter with Hitler, Diana was introduced to him and the month after that, Mosley himself met his German counterpart. For a man who modelled his movement so closely on Hitler's Nazis, Mosley's actual contact with Hitler was scant. In fact they only met twice: once in late April 1935 for an hour's private conversation followed by a lunch with other guests in Hitler's Munich apartment, and once the following year, when Hitler would be guest of honour at Mosley's wedding to Diana.

Mosley, temperamentally unable to be a follower, showed few signs of the grovelling adulation for Hitler displayed by so many other foreign visitors who came to pay court to Germany's new master. Lloyd George and the former King Edward VIII would be far more fulsome in their praise for Hitler's 'achievements' when they met him; but Mosley kept his distance. If Hitler was sounding him out as a possible puppet ruler of Britain in the event of war, he must have been disappointed. Whatever his faults, Mosley was no-one's marionette.

By contrast, Diana was an uncritical worshipper. Her many later admirers, blinded by the usual British sentimentality towards anyone, however repulsive, who totters into extreme old age, have portrayed this unrepentant old Nazi as merely misguided, and have sought to pass off her lifelong admiration for the Nazi leader as an eccentricity or youthful enthusiasm. In truth, Diana was Mosley's *eminence grise* at Hitler's court. She remained, virtually alone in Britain, an apologist for the worst excesses of Nazism – including the Holocaust – to the end of her very long life. Even Mosley, in his later years, seemed somewhat sheepish about Hitler, teasing Diana over her unremitting admiration for him.

As to the substance of the two men's sole private conversation, we only have Mosley's account and a brief reference in the diary of

Joseph Goebbels, Hitler's propaganda chief, a jealous and unreliable source. Goebbels, a guest at the lunch that followed the meeting noted that Mosley: '... makes a good impression. A bit brash, which he tries to conceal behind a forced pushiness. Otherwise acceptable however. Of course, he's on his best behaviour. The Führer has set to work on him. Wonder if he'll ever come to power.'[112]

Years later, Mosley himself reported that during their meeting – conducted through an interpreter – Hitler first appeared pale and listless, but sprang to life when Mosley said that Germany and Britain must never fight each other again after the First World War, which he compared to two equally matched boxers beating each other into a pulp. Mosley echoed Diana in remarking on Hitler's *feminine charm.* Their views concurred, he said in his memoirs, because rather than being rivals they were pursuing parallel paths. There was no need for Germany and Britain to quarrel, as Germany's vital interests lay on the European continent while Britain's were in maintaining its Empire. Hitler agreed. Germany was the leading land power, he said, and Britain the top naval power. Their interests were complementary and should never clash. Mosley called Hitler a *calm and cool customer*; ruthless, but not neurotic. He too echoed Diana in seeing Hitler as a hoot: the Führer and Goebbels shared an *almost exaggerated* sense of humour, he said, with Hitler specialising in mimicry. He would mime himself as a young down and out rolling a cigarette containing a single tobacco shred; and then take off Mussolini, rolling his eyes in the manner of the Italian dictator. Such self-mockery, in Mosley's view, meant that Hitler was wholly sane: *paranoiacs do not make fun of themselves.*[113]

To the lunch Hitler had invited guests with English connections: Unity Mitford, whom he appeared not to realise was already an intimate of Mosley; Winifred Wagner, the English-born daughter-in-law of Hitler's favourite composer; and the Princess of Brunswick, a daughter of the Kaiser. Diana continued to cultivate Hitler and his circle, despite the envious suspicions of some of its members, who affected to believe that she was an agent of Britain's intelligence services. She took care to keep on good terms with the malicious Goebbels and his wife Magda. Sometimes, when staying in Berlin, Diana would be summoned to the Chancellery by Hitler and would find herself in long tête-à-tête meetings with the insomniac Führer into the small hours. As she told her stepson Nicholas, they often found themselves dissolving into paroxysms of laughter together.

Diana was less successful, however, in securing the ostensible aim of her long sojourns in Germany: obtaining financial support for the BUF to replace the dwindling Italian funding, and interesting the Nazis in Mosley's commercial radio schemes. The gossipy Goebbels recorded in his diary in June 1936 that Diana and Unity had asked him to give £100,000 to the cash-strapped British fascists. This had been turned down, but Goebbels had approved a donation of £10,000, still a substantial sum – about £250,000 in today's values. When Diana returned that August to see the Berlin Olympics she requested more cash, but Goebbels, with Hitler's approval, turned her down. To earn the Nazis' support, Goebbels wrote patronisingly, 'Mosley must work harder and be less mercenary.'

In 1937, Diana was in Berlin again to rattle the BUF begging bowl. But Goebbels refused her once more, contemptuously describing Mosley as 'a busted flush' who was 'spending a fortune and getting nowhere'[114] – this despite Goebbels having hosted the wedding of Diana and Mosley from his Berlin flat the previous year. Venting her frustration, Diana let fly with one of the worst insults in the fascist lexicon. It would be easier, she told Nicholas, to get money out of the Jews than to prise it from the tight fists of Nazis like Goebbels.

The Battle of Cable Street

If the BUF's history was plotted on a graph it would fall into three distinct phases. The first, which might be called 'the Italian era' lasted from 1932 to late 1934. The second, 'the German era', was a trough between two peaks, lasting from late 1934 to 1938.

The third and final phase, 'the pacifist era', lasted from 1938 until the movement was banned and its leaders interned in mid-1940. This period was marked by a partial recovery in membership, with recruitment of older and more middle class members; and strong opposition to the growing threat of war with Germany. This chimed in well with the popularity of parallel pacifist movements, particularly supported by ex-servicemen who wished to avoid a second struggle with Germany, and even by the BUF's most bitter enemies, the Communist Party, after the Hitler–Stalin pact of 1939. For a short while, Communists and fascists marched in tandem in the cause of peace.

> The Hitler–Stalin pact (1939) was the starting signal for the second world war. Negotiated in Moscow by Joachim von Ribbentrop, Hitler's foreign minister, and Vyacheslav Molotov, his Russian counterpart, its secret protocols agreed to divide Poland between Germany and the Soviet Union. The pact bewildered Nazis and Communists alike, but within weeks Germany invaded Poland and the Second World War had begun. In June 1941, Hitler tore up the pact and attacked an unprepared Russia.

The swift decline in the BUF's fortunes in 1934–35 had a corrosive effect on the movement. A slackening of internal discipline

THE PACIFIST ERA 109

Mosley in Blackshirt uniform

meant that many recruits strayed from Mosley's Platonic ideal of the new fascist man while the BUF's national headquarters descended into factional squabbling and financial sleaze.

MI5 were not the only intelligence agency that kept a watchful eye on the struggling movement. A Nazi agent named Colin Ross reported to Hitler in 1936 that Mosley's charisma as a leader was no substitute for his movement's organisational disorder. Always a poor judge of character, he tended to listen to the most persuasive flatterer, while the fissures in British fascism widened into chasms.

Mosley did, however, ask Major-General J F C 'Boney' Fuller to put his military mind to making the BUF's policies and publicity more effective. Fuller reported that the loss of the Rothermere press's support could actually benefit the BUF, since newspapers inevitably demanded paybacks as the price of their backing. Such compromises with Rothermere's conservatism, said Fuller, would have bled away the movement's vitality. Fuller cautioned against the unruly excesses of the youthful Blackshirts and fascism's extremist ideology which, he warned, were alienating the conservative British public: 'For every one man and woman who applauds the words "revolution" and "dictatorship" there are ten who actively dislike them . . . Though the wearing of the black shirt appeals to young people . . . this is an old country, very solid, stable and matter of fact . . . the mass of the people will always listen to men and women of experience and importance, but they will seldom listen to boys and girls.'[115]

Mosley responded to this critique by paring down the movement. A K Chesterton was despatched to the provinces to purge BUF branches of members who treated its clubhouses as drinking dens, or, in his words, 'part thieves kitchen and part bawdy houses';[116] and the expensive Black House was given up in the summer of 1935 for a more modest HQ in Great Smith Street. But the chaos inside the movement continued. People mesmerised by Mosley's oratory who signed up to the BUF after one of his meetings would typically not hear from national HQ and would drift away. Only the bedrock of fanatical fascist ideologues, rootless ex-military men and youths out for a scrap, remained.

Mosley did not let his commitment to the movement stand in the way of the playboy lifestyle he had always pursued. The summer holidays of 1935 were again divided between the women he called his 'two wives' – Baba and Diana – and spent in Italy. En route, he was again received in Rome by Mussolini and stood on a podium with the Duce to review a fascist parade. Mosley's children were with him in Italy, gradually getting used to the presence of 'Mrs Guinness'.

Diana was in a delicate condition that summer. In July she had suffered severe facial injuries in a car crash, breaking her nose and jaw, and it was feared that her famously porcelain features would be permanently scarred by inept stitching after the accident.

Skilful plastic surgery saved the day, however, and by the time she departed for her annual visit to the Nuremberg rally in September, her beauty was as flawless as ever. In addition to the accident, Diana also had an abortion to terminate her first pregnancy by Mosley. The experience concentrated her mind: she determined that she wanted to have children by her lover, and to do that she would have to marry him.

Early in 1936, Mosley agreed to their engagement, and Diana set about looking for a suitable country home. Denham, where Mosley's children with Cimmie continued to live in their school holidays, had never been welcoming terrain for her. Instead, Diana rented Wootton Lodge in Staffordshire, near the ancestral estate where Mosley had grown up, and convenient for the North and Midlands where he spent much time on BUF speaking tours. Wootton was an exquisitely beautiful 17th-century house, which reminded Nicholas Mosley of an enchanted castle in a fairy tale, and suggested to others a doll's house. Diana tastefully furnished the rooms and created at once a love nest and a refuge from the growing storms outside.

From 1935, Mosley concentrated his dwindling resources on expanding his following in the East End – where a popular local fascist leader, the young 'Mick' Clarke, a charismatic street corner orator, had emerged. This fascist activity was met with equally active opposition. The local branches of the Communist Party, in which Jewish influence was strong, formed 'fronts' to campaign against Mosley, and the National Council for Civil Liberties monitored fascist violence, frequently raising the issue in the House of Commons. (In fact, fascist attacks on Jews and Communists were roughly matched by Jewish and Communist assaults on fascists.) Slogan daubing, window breaking, assaults with clubs wrapped in barbed wire, and street fights between Blackshirts and their opponents became commonplace.

Meanwhile, Mosley's anti-Semitism was becoming more open and ugly. In March 1936, he told another BUF's rally in the Royal Albert Hall that it was *the intention of fascism to break for ever the power of the Jews in Britain*,[117] and threatened that Jews who did not accept the new order after the BUF had come to power would be deported.

In June, the 'New Press' SS-style uniform of the BUF leadership was unveiled. Mosley and his lieutenants A K Chesterton and Neil Francis Hawkins, were dressed in black, complete with peaked caps, jackboots, jodhpurs, and belted and buttoned military tunics. They marched to a mass rally in Victoria Park, Bow, in the heart of the East End, where Mosley announced that the BUF would put up candidates in the London County Council elections the following year.

Mosley in the 'New Press' uniform

Along with the new uniforms, Mosley changed the name of his movement to the British Union of Fascists and National Socialists (usually shortened to British Union or BU) and, reflecting the withdrawal of Italian funding, changed its emblem from the Italian *Fasces* to a swastika-like symbol of a lightning flash inside a circle, to represent *action inside the circle of comradeship*,[118] but gleefully dubbed by its opponents 'the flash in the pan'.[119]

Mosley spent the rest of the summer recovering from an operation for appendicitis and convalescing at Sorrento in Italy. Meanwhile, fascist activity in the East End was kept at fever pitch, with the BU's star speakers William Joyce, John Beckett,

'Mick' Clarke and Alexander Raven Thomson addressing impromptu street corner meetings. Young Blackshirts marched menacingly through the streets yelling rhythmically 'The Yids! The Yids! We've got to get rid of the Yids!'; the new 'flash in the pan' symbol was chalked and painted everywhere, along with the anti-Semitic slogan 'Perish Judah'; and the columns of *The Blackshirt* and *Fascist Week* were taken up with debates about where the Jews should be expelled to – Palestine or Madagascar being the destinations most frequent suggested.

In the autumn, when Mosley returned after his two-month convalescence, the BU announced plans for a monster rally on Sunday 4 October to capitalise on its East End support. The plan was for Mosley to march through the area, stopping to speak in Shoreditch, Limehouse, Bow and Bethnal Green. In response, anti-fascists, including Jewish, Communist and Labour organisations, drew up a 77,000 signature petition calling for a ban on the march. The government, which had previously attempted to turn a blind eye to the spiralling fascist and anti-fascist violence in the East End, realised that the threat of serious disorder on London's streets could no longer be ignored.

The Commissioner of the Metropolitan Police, Sir Philip Game, drafted in 6,000 officers to keep the two sides apart. In any case, Mosley's contingent of 2,000–3,000 fascists was dwarfed by the crowds – estimated at 100,000 – of anti-fascists who had gathered to bar his path.

As the uniformed BU columns waited in disciplined ranks between the Tower of London and the Royal Mint, their route into the East End was blocked by crowds who had broken into a builder's yard, armed themselves with brickbats, and thrown barricades across Cable Street, Mosley's intended route into the East End. Mosley arrived in his open-topped Bentley in full uniform, and inspected his troops, standing stiffly to attention as the chants of the hostile mob echoed around them. A gang of East

End toughs, led by the Jewish mobster Jack 'Spot' Common, fought their way towards the Bentley to 'get Mosley' and the day's first arrests were made.

The police tried to clear a route for Mosley's marchers. They doggedly fought their way along Cable Street through each barricade, pelted by bricks, bottles and ball bearings. The police responded by drawing truncheons and charging their tormentors, aided by colleagues on horseback. But after two wearying hours, 83 arrests and more than 100 wounded – almost all police and anti-fascists – Cable Street remained uncleared. Sir Philip Game then telephoned the Home Secretary, Sir John Simon, to ask permission to call the march off. 'As you can see for yourself,' Game told Mosley, 'if you fellows go ahead from here there will be a

Mosley at Mint Street Rally displaying the fascist salute and SS uniforms

shambles. I am not going to have that. You must call it off.' Mosley asked: *Is that an order?*[120] and when told that it was, he turned his men round and marched west through deserted Sunday streets to Charing Cross pier, where he dismissed them with a speech of defiance.

'The Battle of Cable Street' entered left-wing mythology as a famous victory over fascism, waged by a heroic, politically engaged populace. Mosley angrily accused the government of capitulating to mob rule and Communist violence in failing to assert the fascists' right to free speech. Both versions distorted the truth. If there had been a battle, it had been exclusively between the police and the anti-fascists, an outcome that Mosley had ensured by ordering his troops to stand aside from the clashes. The fascists, in fact, had shirked a struggle of their own making. But truth did not stand in the way of the essential myth of Cable Street: that Mosley had tried to march through the East End – and had failed humiliatingly. Once again, as at Olympia, in the eyes of the British public and 'respectable' opinion, Mosley's fascism had been indelibly tainted with the stain of violent thuggery.

Mosley, however, did not wait for the post-mortem. The day after Cable Street, on 5 October 1936, he secretly flew to join Diana in Berlin. The following day they were married in the drawing room of the Nazi propaganda minister, Joseph Goebbels, and his wife Magda. The guest of honour was Hitler.

Marginalisation of a Movement

Even for the sublimely self-confident Mosley, a wedding hosted by the top Nazi hierarchy was a bizarre notion. Believing that he could keep the news secret, and that it would not damage him even if it leaked out, is testimony to Mosley's arrogance and to his curious half-contact with reality. For all his protestations of keeping his distance from Hitler, Mosley acquiesced to Diana's scheme for the Führer to be part of one of the most solemn moments of their lives. The idea for the Nazi nuptials had been first floated by Magda Goebbels the previous month, eagerly taken up by Diana – who saw it as a way of avoiding unwelcome publicity at home – and agreed to by Goebbels and Hitler, despite their doubts over Mosley's viability as Britain's future fascist dictator.

The wedding ceremony was attended only by Hitler, the registrar, the Goebbels, a radiantly happy Unity, and by Mosley's two witnesses, the MI5 'mole' W E D 'Bill' Allen, and Captain Gordon-Canning, a friend from Mosley's former regiment. After a wedding lunch given by the Goebbels at their suburban lakeside home, the party adjourned to the Berlin Sportspalast stadium where a crowd of 20,000 heard Hitler decry democracy and decadence. It was the first time that Mosley had witnessed Hitler's hypnotic oratory, and despite barely understanding German, it must have been an instructive experience for a fellow fascist orator hoping to emulate his Nazi counterpart's success.

Following a formal dinner hosted by Hitler at the Chancellery, the two men parted, never to meet again. Hitler boarded his special train for Munich, while the newly-weds repaired to the Kaiserhof Hotel for their honeymoon night, which degenerated into a nagging quarrel. The next day they flew home. Despite subsequent embarrassment over the peculiar circumstances of the wedding, the event paid off in the short term, in that no word of the ceremony appeared in the tightly-controlled, Goebbels-run German media, while beyond a small family circle, their secret remained safe in England, too. Only gradually did it become known that Mosley and Diana were married, and even then the exact circumstances of their wedding remained obscure.

Meanwhile, the echoes of Cable Street continued to reverberate. Defiantly demonstrating that the East End remained his stronghold, Mosley addressed a series of public meetings there on returning from Germany. On 11 October 1936, he spoke to 12,000 in Victoria Park, and led a march through Limehouse, repeating the exercise in Shoreditch on 14 October. 'A definite pro-fascist feeling has manifested itself . . . since the events of 4th October . . .' a Special Branch report concluded. 'It is reliably reported that the London membership [of the BU] has increased by 2,000.'[121]

A week after Cable Street, in the so-called 'Mile End Road Pogrom' a gang of young fascist thugs smashed Jewish shop windows in scenes resembling the Nazi takeover in Germany. Alarmed by these events, the National Government took the advice of the Labour leader of the London County Council, Herbert Morrison, an old foe of Mosley's, and introduced the Public Order Bill into the Commons and it became law on 1 January 1937. The Act seriously inhibited the BU's ability to organise meetings and generate publicity. Mosley had challenged the liberal state – and the liberal state had hit back. Nevertheless, fascist meetings and marches continued to be a noisy feature of British life in the late 1930s.

However, the passing of the Act was overshadowed by the abdication crisis. The relationship of the new King Edward VIII with the twice-divorced American socialite Mrs Wallis Simpson had long been known to the social circles in which they moved and was openly discussed in the foreign media. But in an era when global communications were still in their infancy, the wider British public remained ignorant of their popular monarch's amorous activities.

Edward's vague remark that 'something must be done'[122] after visiting the depressed coalfields of South Wales late in 1936, increased his popularity with the working classes, though middle-class, Anglican and non-conformist opinion looked askance at his playboy image. Crucially, the government, in the shape of Prime Minister Stanley Baldwin, regarded Edward as a menace. The King's carelessness with secret papers and his reluctance to buckle down to his royal duties were matched by his open sympathy with the Nazi 'experiment' in Germany. At a time when war clouds were gathering, a fascist-minded monarch was at best an embarrassment, at worst a danger to the state. With a compliant and safely married brother on hand to succeed, and Edward still uncrowned, the King's obsession with Mrs Simpson offered the perfect excuse to ease him off the throne. In December 1936, Baldwin issued an ultimatum: Edward would have to choose between his mistress and the throne.

The pro-fascist sympathy that made the King so suspect to the

> The Public Order Act outlawed paramilitary uniforms and increased police powers to ban, reroute and control marches and demonstrations. Thus, the Act removed the power of the BU to police their own meetings and eliminated the propagandist value of uniforms. Though the fascists complained that the Act curbed the right to wear whatever clothes one liked and parade wherever one pleased, Mosley was aware that in donning the new black uniform he had pushed things too far. *The old soldier in me*, he ruefully admitted, *got the better of the politician.*

The Duke and Duchess of Windsor photographed after their marriage in 1936

government naturally made him equally attractive to Mosley. The two men moved in the same social circles. 'Fruity' Metcalfe, Edward's future best man, was the husband of Baba Metcalfe, Mosley's ex-sister-in-law and mistress. Seeking a populist issue to revive the BU's faltering fortunes, the abdication crisis looked like a godsend to Mosley and, with his fellow mavericks Churchill and Beaverbrook, he briefly toyed with the idea of forming a 'King's party' as a stick with which to beat Baldwin and the stuffed shirts of the National Government.

When the crisis burst, Mosley summoned William Joyce and John Beckett, respectively the BU's directors of propaganda and publications, from London to a suite at Liverpool's Adelphi Hotel. According to Beckett, they found the Leader in a state of excitement bordering on mania. Mosley claimed to have been in touch with the King, who had apparently told him that he would defy Baldwin, accept the government's resignation and appoint Mosley as Prime Minister in his place. Pacing the room, Mosley outlined his plans to rule without parliament until an election had been organised, during which he would broadcast to the nation and swing public opinion behind fascism. The meeting was interrupted by a telephone call which Mosley conducted in a code he had first used in his schooldays, in order, he said, to circumvent the intelligence agencies who bugged his calls. Beckett recalled:

'I am sure that Mosley really believed he was on the threshold of great power. The conversation confirmed my suspicion that he was deluded, and was dangerously near the borderline between genius and insanity. I knew the man to whom he had spoken. He was a dilettante society friend of Mosley, who lived in as fictitious a world of grandeur as Mosley himself . . . '[123]

Nevertheless, Beckett retained enough respect for the Leader to obediently organise a BU 'Stand by the King' campaign. Beckett wrote pamphlets, ran street-chalking groups and edited a special newspaper, *Crisis*. But the campaign – along with Mosley's perpetually revived hopes that he was about to be summoned to power – collapsed before it had got off the ground. It was stymied by the King's capitulation to Baldwin's ultimatum.

Mosley heard Edward's abdication broadcast at Wootton, and though he railed at the government for a *flagrant act of dictatorship*[124] in forcing the king from the throne, he knew that the marital difficulties of a modern monarch would hardly summon the people to the barricades. In later life, the Mosleys remained close to the Windsors. They shared a long Parisian exile for decades after the Second World War, and Diana would write a biography of Wallis Simpson – perhaps from shared feelings as an adventuress who had defied convention, gambled for the highest stakes – and lost.

In 1937, Mosley concentrated on the London County Council elections in the BU's East End bastion. The campaign was shamelessly populist and patriotic. Mosley pledged to pull down slum houses and replace them with modern blocks funded by public money. The BU countered the slogan 'Vote Labour and save Madrid' with 'Vote British Union and save London', and promised that no more money would be spent on housing the asylum-seekers of the day Basque refugees from the Spanish Civil War. BU candidates, including Joyce, Beckett, Clarke and Raven

Thomson — stood in three boroughs: Bethnal Green, Limehouse and Shoreditch, but despite the money and resources that the movement poured in, the results, in March 1937, were disappointing. The average BU vote in the three boroughs fell just short of 20 per cent, less than half the total of their victorious Labour opponents.

Mosley strove to put a brave face on the results. As they came in, he sat down with pencil and paper and triumphantly declared that the BU percentage was higher than Hitler had won for the Nazis in his first big electoral test in 1930. Mosley told a German newspaper: *Our struggle against the Jews . . . has helped us to win . . . Britain and Germany must be in the closest possible alliance.*[125]

The BU's failure to make significant headway even in its East End heartland had one immediate consequence: costs had to be slashed. With Italian subsidies finally at an end and German replacements failing to match them, the BU's pretensions to be a nationwide political party with a headquarters and apparatus to match, were clearly unsustainable. Five days after the elections, Mosley summarily sacked Joyce and Beckett as salaried officials, along with most of their colleagues. The BU's payroll was decimated from 143 to just 30. Effective control of the movement now rested in the pudgy hands of Neil Francis Hawkins, who saw it as a paramilitary elite force rather than a mass political party. Increasingly, Mosley distanced himself from the ever-more shambolic running of his movement, spending his time, like an ageing rock star, in ceaseless 'concert tour' speaking engagements.

John Beckett, who had been heard by an MI5 mole inside the movement on election night inveighing against Mosley's 'credulous complacency' and the 'idiocy and incompetence' of those around him, noted that the long list of those fired, besides Beckett and Joyce, included 'every other man or woman on his staff who had ever reasoned with or contradicted him or his henchmen'.[126] Beckett had good reason to be bitter: he was an able journalist who had turned the dwindling circulations of *Action* and *The Blackshirt* around, only to see his work wasted in petty backbiting among the band of pencil-moustached Mosley lookalikes who now surrounded the Leader. He put his finger on the real reason behind Mosley's mini-Night of the Long Knives: Mosley's pathological vanity, his pompous, self-important humourlessness – though he was still capable of schoolboy japes within his own family circle – and his hauteur as the undisputed Leader, were all offended by the irreverence and independence of Joyce and Beckett.

After the Second World War, Mosley suggested, disingenuously, that it was the two men's extreme anti-Semitism which had caused him to purge them. But he made no mention of this in his public explanations for the cull at the time – blaming it purely on the urgent need to economise.

Mosley's own language regarding the Jews was scarcely less inflammatory than the gutter oratory of his two unruly lieutenants. Such statements as *the sweepings of the continental ghettos hired by Jewish financiers*; *Jewish rascals*; the *yelping of a Yiddish mob*[127] and his habitual references to *alien forces* and *alien faces* were hardly those of a fastidious statesman spurning anti-Semitism. During the London elections of 1937, Mosley had made a clear pitch for the anti-Semitic vote, pledging that he would send the Jews *back to where they belong* and that he would replace notices to quit from Jewish landlords to their tenants by giving the Jews themselves notice to quit Britain.

Increasingly, Mosley reacted to the slightest criticism with insensate fury. When John McNab, an acolyte of Joyce, dared to protest at his friend's purging, Mosley thumped his desk, and roared that Joyce was a traitor whom he would *roll in blood*[128] and smash, and that anyone who dared defend him was a traitor too. McNab was then escorted from the BU's HQ by a fascist heavy.

In the wake of the elections and the purge, Mosley was presiding over a visibly declining force. The difficulty of hiring halls after the Public Order Act meant that fascist meetings were usually held in the open, with lower attendance, less money from ticket sales and more violence. In 1937, a jagged brick hit Mosley on the head in Liverpool, laying him low for a week.

Formerly a famously successful litigant, Mosley suffered the humiliation in a libel case of being awarded damages of a farthing, the lowest sum possible, against the *News Chronicle* which had accused him of advocating the use of machine guns against opponents. *Action* was bankrupted by the award of £20,000 damages in another libel case brought by the owner of the *Daily Telegraph*, Lord Camrose, against the erstwhile editor of *Action*, John Beckett, who had incautiously accused him of being a Jew. Disillusion spread, and there were more resignations from the BU's leadership. Charles Wegg-Prosser and Jim Bailey, high profile candidates in the London County Council elections, both quit, followed by A K Chesterton, who cited Mosley's retreat from reality as the reason for his resignation: 'Flops are written up as triumphs, and enormous pains are taken . . . to give the impression of strength where there is weakness, growth where there is decline, of influence where there is only indifference.'[129]

Mosley recuperating after being struck by a brick in Liverpool 1937

'Minding Britain's Business'

It was hardly surprising that Mosley retreated from this desolate scene by spending more time with his two families at his two country houses – Denham and Wootton. His visits to Denham, where his three children by Cimmie were being brought up by their aunts Irene and Baba, were increasingly fraught occasions. Wootton, by contrast, was a haven from the rough and tumble of fascist street politics. Serenaded by the music of Wagner, Mosley could read, write and enjoy the traditional country pursuits of shooting and riding. His daughter Vivien and second son Mickey were neglected by their father, but his eldest son, Nicholas, now a gawky Etonian, would shuttle between Denham and Wootton, and even, in the summer of 1937, accompanied Mosley to the BU's summer camp near Selsey in Sussex. Nicholas, a sceptical youth, argued with Diana about Hitler's Germany, but still deferred to his distant, troubling father.

In autumn 1937, Mosley visited Germany seeking sponsorship for Air Time, a company he had formed to implement his plan to broadcast radio propaganda into Britain. By patient negotiation and discreet lobbying of Hitler, Diana had succeeded in securing German agreement to sponsor the proposed station, only for her plans to eventually be scuppered by the war.

Despite his happiness with her, Diana's family caused Mosley endless embarrassment. Unity continued as a member of Hitler's circle, not realising that she was being used as a tool in intrigues among the Führer's courtiers. Such plots could prove lethal to the

A well-attended BUF rally in Bermondsey 1936

losers. In one, Unity's tactlessness nearly brought about the destruction of her original conduit into Hitler's circle: 'Putzi' Hanfstängel. Some gossip from her to the Führer about Hanfstängel's mild criticism of the regime, ended with Putzi being driven into exile, and he only narrowly escaped with his life. Diana and Unity's parents, Lord and Lady Redesdale, and their brother, Tom were by now enthusiastic Hitler-worshippers and leading lights in some of the many influential pro-German British groups and clubs such as the Link, the Anglo-German Fellowship, the Nordic League and the Right Club which, funded by German gold, were agitating against the approaching war.

Not all the Mitfords were Nazis, however. Jessica ('Decca') and her husband Esmond Romilly were ardent Communists active on the anti-fascist side in the Spanish Civil War. The eldest sister, Nancy, had put herself beyond the pale with the Mosleys by writing a satirical novel *Wigs on the Green* (1935) in which she mercilessly mocked the BU as 'the Union Jackshirts' led by their POF (Poor Old Führer) 'Colonel Jack'. Although Nancy cut three chapters lampooning Mosley, influenced by his reputation as a litigant, and redirected her fire against her sister Unity, the book deeply offended both Mosley and Diana.

An even wittier spoof of Mosley and his movement came from P G Wodehouse, who, in *The Code of the Woosters* (1938) poked fun at Mosley, as 'Roderick Spode', leader of the 'Saviours of Britain', otherwise known as the 'Black Shorts' for their uniform of black football shorts. Bertie Wooster tells Spode some uncomfortable home truths: 'Just because you have succeeded in inducing a handful of half-wits to disfigure the London scene by going about in black shorts, you think you're someone. You hear them shouting "Heil Spode!" and you imagine it is the Voice of the People. That is where you make your bloomer. What the Voice of the People is saying is: "Look at that frightful ass Spode swanking about in footer bags! Did you ever in your puff see such a perfect perisher?"'[130]

Ironically, Wodehouse, an essentially apolitical Francophile, would be exposed to the unfunny side of fascism during the Second World War, when, trapped in France in 1940 by the rapid German advance, he was lured to Berlin and made some unwise broadcasts on Nazi radio for which he was heavily criticised in Britain, and which led him to spend the rest of his life in the United States.

Mosley spent the winter of 1937–38 at Wootton convalescing and writing *Tomorrow We Live*, a fascist tract in which he declared himself a *National Socialist*[131] and pointed to Jewish financial clout as the main enemy of the British empire. The Jews, Marx and Freud were singled out for attack: Marx for his materialism; Freud for his determinism. With its defiant insistence on the primacy of will over circumstance, the book reflected the position of Mosley's embattled movement: cash-strapped, marginalised and denied the oxygen of publicity.

The year 1938 was dominated by the inexorable approach of war. The Anschluss takeover of Austria by Hitler's Germany in March, accompanied by the open persecution of Vienna's Jews, was followed by Hitler's growing hate campaign against Czechoslovakia, with Nazi demands for the dismemberment of the state and the annexation of the German-populated Sudetenland.

Mosley reacted by ordering the BU to mount a 'Peace Campaign' under the slogans: 'Britons fight for Britain only' and 'Mosley for Peace'. At first the campaign struck a chord with public opinion. Until the Munich conference in October 1938, at which Prime Minister Neville Chamberlain, who had succeeded Baldwin the previous year, wrote a blank cheque for Hitler to tear up Czechoslovakia, public opinion broadly favoured meeting 'reasonable' German demands in Eastern Europe. There was a feeling that Germany had been unjustly treated after the First World War, and that in absorbing German-speaking territories Hitler was merely 'going into his own backyard'.

The BU successfully tapped into this mood, and its membership, which had hit a low of around 5,000, saw a modest revival up to about 10,000, mainly middle-class people worried by the threat of war.

The Munich conference proved a watershed, however, as did the Kristallnacht pogroms of the following month, in which scores of Jews were murdered and beaten, synagogues torched and shops and businesses trashed by officially-sponsored mobs across Germany.

British public opinion began to shift. There was widespread sympathy with the victims of Nazi persecution, as the bestial nature of Hitler's regime became apparent to more and more people. These opinions hardened in March 1939 when Hitler's armies marched into the rump of Czechoslovakia, to oppress a non-German people. The mass of moderate opinion, however

A major BUF rally at Earls Court 1936

reluctantly, faced up to the increasing certainty of war with an implacably expansionist Germany.

Nonetheless, even as Germany began a familiar campaign of threats against its next target, Poland, a substantial minority remained adamantly opposed to war at any price. On 16 July 1939, up to 20,000 filled London's Earl's Court stadium in what Mosley boasted was Britain's biggest-ever indoor political meeting, to hear his message of peace. The hall was festooned with giant banners proclaiming 'MIND BRITAIN'S BUSINESS' and this now-familiar BU slogan still contained the kernel of Mosley's message. *We will have no part in your Jews' quarrel,*[132] he told the crowd. Britain should stand aloof from the gathering storm. It was a message, however, that as the summer of 1939 wore on, fell on deaf ears.

War and Internment

The last weeks of peace ebbed hopelessly away for the Mosleys. The couple had been forced to publicly announce their marriage in November 1938 when Diana gave birth to their first son, Alexander. The following summer she was once again in Germany with Unity, attending the Bayreuth Wagner festival as Hitler's guests. On the festival's final day, the Führer summoned the two sisters for a private talk, telling them gloomily that England seemed set on war. Diana told him of Mosley's campaign for peace, and Hitler warned that unless he was careful her husband would share the fate of Jean Jaurès, the French socialist leader assassinated on the eve of war in 1914 for his passionate advocacy of peace.

At the outbreak of war on 3 September 1939, the Mosleys were in London, listening to Neville Chamberlain's funereal voice on the radio declaring war. Diana's foremost concern was for Unity, still in Germany. In October, the news arrived that Diana had most dreaded. On the day war broke out, Unity had shot herself in the head in a Munich park. Miraculously, she survived, and Hitler had her repatriated.

Mosley ordered BU members not to hinder the war effort, whatever their private feelings. He continued to hold public meetings calling for peace. But the increasing unpopularity of the BU was vividly demonstrated when it scored a derisory 3 per cent in two parliamentary by-elections in which it fielded 'peace' candidates. At one of these, Mosley was assaulted by an angry crowd.

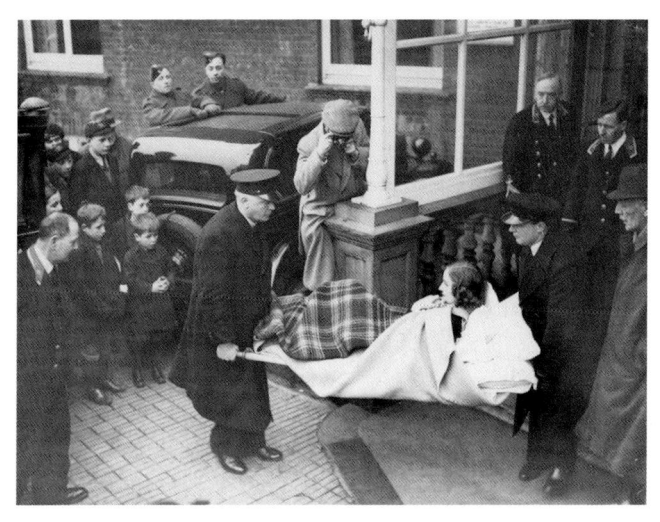

An injured Unity Mitford is returned to England 1939

Privately, Mosley was meeting secretly with like-minded members of fascist, anti-Semitic and pro-Nazi groups to discuss possible co-operation.

Britain's fascists had been fractured by the war. Some, such as A K Chesterton and Tom Mitford, decided that their primary loyalty was to Britain and joined the forces. Others waged a covert campaign for a peace that would accept Nazi domination of Europe, stealing out at night to paste up peace posters. A few, like William Joyce, actually left the country to join the enemy.

In early 1940, the Mosleys gave up Wootton, dividing their time between Denham and a flat in London's Dolphin Square. In April, Diana gave birth to her second child by Mosley, a boy named Max. The following month, with the German armies poised to attack in the west, Mosley printed a statement in *Action* on 9 May urging his followers to resist any attempt to invade Britain: *However rotten the existing government, and however much we detested its policies, we would throw ourselves into the effort of a united nation until the foreigner was driven from our soil. In such a situation no doubt exists concerning the attitude of British Union.*[133] Mosley was putting it on record that he refused to play the traitor's role of Vidkun Quisling, the Norwegian Nazi leader who had recently formed a puppet government after the German occupation of his country. The next day, as the Blitzkrieg swept through France and the Low Countries, Winston Churchill replaced Chamberlain as Prime Minister, and tough times began for the Mosleys and their fellow British fascists.

Mosley believed that he would have been 'bumped off' by Britain's security services in the event of an invasion. He was well aware that his movement was riddled with spies but he regarded the surveillance as a joke, reasoning that he had nothing to hide – except, of course, for his foreign financing which he took great pains to conceal, though in vain. He also hoped to convert naturally right-wing MI5 officers to fascism.

The penetration of the BU by the security services meant that they knew where the key fascist figures lived should there ever be a mass round-up. The government had armed itself with such draconian powers as soon as the war had begun, and under the notorious Defence Regulation 18(b) had the power to suspend habeas corpus and trial by jury and intern suspects indefinitely should they be thought to threaten the state.

The trigger that caused the new government to invoke these powers of detention, despite a lack of hard evidence that Britain's fascists would aid and abet the enemy, was a spy scandal involving not Mosley's movement, but a small fringe fascist group. Anna Wolkoff, a White Russian emigré and a fanatical fascist belonging to Archibald Maule Ramsay's Right Club, was found to be communicating to the Italian embassy documents stolen by Tyler Kent, a right-wing cipher clerk at the US embassy. When Kent's flat was raided, 1,500 stolen ciphers were found, including transcripts of top secret telephone conversations between Churchill and President Roosevelt, in which Churchill urged the US to intervene in the war on the Allied side. If such correspondence had found their way into the American newspapers, Roosevelt might not have been re-elected in a strongly isolationist US, Churchill could have fallen and the war might have been lost. The stakes could hardly have been higher. Mosley was known to have been in at least indirect contact with Ramsay's Right Club, so, taking no chances, the government cracked down.

On the evening of 23 May 1940, Mosley and Diana were driving to Dolphin Square from Denham. They saw five men standing, apparently aimlessly, outside their flat. 'Look, coppers,'[134] Diana remarked. The detectives explained that Mosley was being detained under 18(b) and would be taken straight to Brixton prison. Diana drove back to Denham alone, seeing newspaper placards en route proclaiming the arrest of Archibald Maule Ramsay.

The swoop had also netted the remaining HQ staff of the BU and other leading fascists around Britain. All told, 800 BU members, including 100 women – mainly middle-aged, as many younger members were serving in the forces – were held in filthy conditions in disused prison wings at Brixton, Holloway and Liverpool. The movement had been effectively destroyed, and the subsequent formal banning of the BU in July 1940 was a mere formality.

For the moment, Diana remained at liberty, though she was tailed by police, her homes at Denham and Dolphin Square were searched, and Mosley's shotguns seized. Diana visited Mosley daily at Brixton – he grew a beard, saying that conditions were so verminous that the smallest shaving nick was soon infected. Diana cast around for legal help only to be rejected in turn by the BU's regular lawyer and by Mosley's and her own family solicitors. Suddenly, the Mosleys were dangerous to know for respectable folk with reputations to protect. Ironically, Oswald Hickson, a left-wing lawyer well-versed in taking on civil liberties cases, eventually took the brief, but there was little he could do against an implacable government and a hostile public opinion.

As the battle in France reached its disastrous climax at Dunkirk, Diana experienced the force of panicky public opinion in full cry after scapegoats. As old friends fell by the wayside, she responded with icy disdain. In June, Denham was requisitioned by the government to serve as a chemical warfare experiment station. Two of Mosley's children by Cimmie, Vivien and Mickey, were placed under the legal guardianship of their Aunt Irene, who took them to the safety of Scotland.

Diana Mosley 1940

On the last evening before she was due to leave Denham, Diana was reading in the garden, having arranged for herself and her two infants to stay with her sister Pam near Banbury in Oxfordshire. The family nanny came to report that three policemen and a policewoman had called. It was Diana's turn to be arrested by the state she despised. Assured that she would only be detained for a day or two, Diana insisted on stopping at a chemist en route to Holloway prison to purchase a breast pump, since she was still nursing her baby Max, just 11 weeks old. However, as soon as she arrived at Holloway it became clear that her incarceration would not be brief. The jail was filling with other fascist women, joining the more usual prison clientele of prostitutes, thieves and drunks.

Diana was locked inside a small metal cell to await the humiliating prison ritual of a delousing bath and an inspection for scabies. She was faced with stinking blankets, meals of gristle swimming in grease, or putrid fish pie rejected even by the prison cats, washed down with cocoa so fat that the women skimmed off the top to use as face cream, all served in unwashed tin pans shoved under her cell door. She did not eat for a week, and was constantly afraid of infection from the filth of 'E' wing, which had not been used for a decade. Prison was a rude shock for Diana, for which her privileged life had not remotely prepared her. (Her misery and bitterness would have been compounded had she known that her own sister, Nancy, had gone to see a Foreign Office friend, Gladwyn Jebb, to demand that her 'dangerous' sister should be locked up.)

Meanwhile, Mosley was faring somewhat better than his wife. Housed in 'F' wing at Brixton, his early cell-mates included a black musician unlucky enough to have played with the Berlin Philharmonic Orchestra. Mosley said he found him *a charming and cultured man*.[135] There was also an assortment of fellow fascists. Mosley compared notes with Ramsay, on their accommodation. They stoically agreed that Brixton was no worse than their public schools, or billets on the Western Front. With them was Admiral Sir Barry Domvile, a leading light in the Link, a society dedicated to forging close Anglo-German ties; Harry St John Philby, a harsh critic of British policy in the Middle East and father of the infamous Soviet spy Kim; and Mosley's former comrade turned critic, John Beckett, who had moved to the British People's Party, one of several groups which disguised their fascism under a platform of pacifism; and Arnold Leese, head of the Imperial Fascist League.

Mosley's early months in prison were an agony of frustration for a man addicted to activity. He passed them in bouts of reading. Goethe's *Faust* was his favourite, along with Nietzsche and Schiller, and he learned German to read them in the original. He attempted to keep fit with daily physical exercises, and wrote almost daily letters to Diana full of tender concern for her welfare.

He received visits from his children, family and friends: two of whom, Baba Metcalfe and the Duke of Windsor's former chief adviser, Walter Monckton, were discreetly lobbying for the Mosleys' release.

Prison life was not without its ironies. Detained with the fascists were a number of hapless Italian immigrants, hauled in after Mussolini joined Hitler's war in June. The Italians, including some teenagers, displayed an unheroic attitude when the Blitz on London began. They yelled in fear as the German bombers roared overhead. By contrast, reported the jail's governor, C F Clayton, the BU detainees stood at their cell windows to cheer on RAF fighters attacking the enemy. According to Clayton, Mosley set an example to his followers: 'He followed the exploits of the RAF . . . with intense appreciation of their gallantry, and showed ardent anxiety for their success.'[136]

In 1941, with the Battle of Britain won and the immediate danger of invasion past, conditions for the detainees improved. As political prisoners, the law allowed them certain privileges denied to Brixton's ordinary criminal inmates. The fascists could have food and even alcohol brought in, were allowed to wear their own clothes and were permitted freer association with their fellow detainees. But such comforts were a movable feast: the authorities were apt to remove or restrict privileges in response to hostile press comment about detainees living a life of luxury while Londoners endured the Blitz. Rumours appeared in the papers alleging that Mosley was playing bridge for high stakes, drinking fine wines and champagne, and had his silk underwear and dress suits laundered in the West End.

In December 1940, after parliamentary questions were asked about the detainees, Churchill took time off from running the war to inquire about their conditions. He fired a memo to Mosley's old enemy, the Home Secretary, Herbert Morrison, asking that they be allowed more baths, letters and literature. The Prime

Minister also demanded that Diana should be allowed to see her baby 'from whom she was taken before it was weaned'.

After Churchill's intervention, Mosley was allowed to make monthly visits to Diana in Holloway. She had by now adapted to the rigours of prison in her own style, dining on Stilton cheese sent in from Harrods, and ostentatiously wearing a fur coat. (Ironically, it had been purchased from the proceeds of one of several libel actions that the Mosleys had successfully pursued from prison against press reports that they were living in the lap of luxury.)

The Mosleys benefited from their close relationship with Churchill, reflecting the cosy clubbishness that still dominated Britain's political life. Mosley and Churchill had been parliamentary colleagues and occasional political allies since the First World War. They had stayed in one another's houses, and shared many of the same personal traits and attributes. Both were stirring orators and unreliable party men (unless they were leading the party concerned). Both had repeatedly changed political allegiance. Both were widely distrusted for their egotism and lack of judgement. The major difference between them was that Churchill remained a democrat and a parliamentarian, whereas Mosley held such revered institutions in contempt.

Although many of the Mosleys' well-born friends had distanced themselves from the disgraced couple, a courageous few did not. Bob Boothby, his own political career blighted by financial scandal, visited Mosley in prison, as did Harold Nicolson – now a junior minister in Churchill's government – and Jimmy Maxton, leader of the Independent Labour Party. Via such faithful friends, Mosley was able to lobby for an amelioration in the conditions in which he and his fellow captives were held. He suggested, sensibly enough, that they should do productive agricultural labour on communal farms rather than merely rotting in jail. But, once again, it was only Churchill's personal intervention, overruling

Morrison, which secured improvements. Churchill was, Mosley admitted, *a genial host*[137] during his enforced residence as a guest of the government.

Over time, the internment of Britain's fascists became a legal nightmare for the government. Evidence of treasonable activities or opinions against all but a minority of BU members – Mosley estimated them as 5 per cent of the movement – was negligible, and often acquired by dubious means. At one point, Alexander Raven Thomson and other detained BU members were taken to Ham Common, a secret MI5 interrogation centre where psychological and occasionally physical torture was used on captured German spies. The British fascists were starved and threatened with immediate execution if they would not co-operate with the authorities.

An advisory committee on internment was set up under the Liberal lawyer, Norman Birkett, KC. In July 1940, Birkett grilled Mosley but he survived the forensic examination, firmly rebutting suggestions that he would collaborate with a German invasion, and successfully obfuscating Birkett's attempts to discover the sources of his movement's finances.

In 16 hours of cross-examination, Mosley countered the government's case on every point. Was the BU part of a fascist international movement subservient to Hitler and Mussolini? No, the BU was a British national movement, it was the Labour Party which was part of an international socialist movement. Did his fascists persecute their Jewish and Communist opponents? No, they simply defended themselves when attacked. But Mosley admitted that after studying how the Jews penetrated and controlled British businesses and institutions, he had become an anti-Semite – although that too, was not illegal.

Had his movement been financed from Italy? No, Mosley lied, but even if it had, that too was not illegal. Why had he met Hitler and Mussolini? To exchange views and seek peace; Lloyd George,

George Lansbury and the Duke of Windsor had done the same. Did his peace campaign not undermine the nation's will to fight? No, since the BU put the defence of national interests and the British empire before all else. It was his right to oppose the war, as Lord Chatham had opposed the American War of Independence, Charles James Fox the wars against revolutionary France, and Lloyd George and Ramsay MacDonald the Boer and First World Wars respectively. Above all, Mosley insisted, he was a patriot whose political views were his birthright as an Englishman. With this robust defence, the government's attempt to prove Mosley a traitor collapsed, and they were forced to fall back on reasons of state as the sole grounds for his detention. As the war wore on and the danger of German invasion or Axis victory receded, these grounds proved less and less easy to justify.

Late in 1940, most BU detainees, along with many of the aliens from Axis countries who had also been swept up in the government dragnet, were moved to a camp at Ascot racecourse, thence to a council estate at Huyton near Liverpool and finally to the Isle of Man. By the summer of 1941, of the 671 fascists still held, only 44, including Mosley, remained at Brixton. Diana and 23 other women fascists remained at Holloway.

Baba Metcalfe was especially assiduous in her efforts to free Mosley. In September 1941, her latest beau, Lord Halifax, former Foreign Secretary and now Britain's ambassador to Washington, gave a dinner party for the Churchills at which Baba pleaded her case. Churchill raised no objection to the idea of uniting Mosley and Diana in prison, but warned that Herbert Morrison, with his grudge against Mosley, would be an implacable obstacle.

In November 1941, after dining with Diana's brother Tom Mitford who had also pleaded the Mosleys' case, Churchill sent another memo to Morrison suggesting that the remaining fascist prisoners should be released on parole. Morrison grudgingly responded by allowing Mosley to join Diana in a small block within Holloway. Here, conditions were relatively comfortable. Mosley was allowed to cultivate his own vegetable patch, and Diana permitted to prepare their meals.

However, the move to Holloway proved less than a halfway-house to freedom. The Labour half of Churchill's coalition government was adamantly opposed to 'appeasing' fascists, as Morrison put it, whatever the Prime Minister's own private views. The Mosleys made the best of things, as the prospect of Allied victory grew ever more certain. In their cell block, the Mosleys were bizarrely allowed the use of sex offenders as servants. Their children visited regularly, and were sometimes allowed to stay overnight.

In 1943, Mosley's health deteriorated sharply. The old problems in his legs flared up and developed into serious phlebitis. Mosley's mother called in the royal physician, Lord Dawson of Penn, and other eminent doctors to confirm the diagnosis. Lady Mosley, accompanied by her grandson Nicholas, obtained an interview with Clementine Churchill, a former friend, to press for his release. She was sternly told by the Prime Minister's wife that the Mosleys were better off in jail since they would be in danger from hostile mobs should they be freed. Undaunted, Mosley's friends and family continued lobbying the government, pointing out that with the Allies victorious on every front, whatever danger Mosley had once posed to national security had long since disappeared. Quite suddenly, the government gave in.

In mid-November 1943, it was announced that the Mosleys were being conditionally set free, due to Mosley's ill health and because the danger they posed to national security had vanished. Herbert Morrison told MPs that he had no wish 'to make martyrs of those who did not deserve the honour'.[138] The decision provoked an immediate uproar on the left. Petitions against the release were circulated in workplaces, protest marches were held and angry editorials appeared in the socialist *Daily Herald* and the

Communist *Daily Worker* calling Mosley: 'A symbol of the evil we are fighting against.'[139] Just as Diana's sister Nancy had gone out of her way to have her sister detained, so another Mitford sister, Jessica, embittered by the recent death in action of her husband Esmond Romilly, wrote an open letter to Esmond's cousin Winston Churchill, demanding that the Mosleys stay inside 'where they belong'.

For two days, crowds surged around Holloway with placards proclaiming 'Hang Mosley!' Finally, in the early hours of 16 November, under the cover of a snowstorm, the Mosleys were smuggled out of a side gate in the prison wall and driven to Rignell, the Oxfordshire home of Diana's sister, Pamela, and her husband, the government scientific adviser Derek Jackson, where their children were waiting. Although Mosley was thin, ill and virtually bedridden, he was free for the first time in three-and-a-half years, and surrounded by creature comforts and his young children.

Public opinion clearly displayed in 1943

Fascism Reborn

It was said of the French Bourbons, returning to take up the reins of power after the revolution and the Napoleonic era, that they had 'Learned nothing and forgotten nothing'.[140] The same could be said of Mosley. At first, he and Diana were hedged around with strict restrictions. Effectively, they remained under house arrest. Forbidden to reside in or visit London, they had to inform the authorities of where they lived. Public speaking, publishing, journalism or contact with former political associates was banned. The government was gagging Mosley.

For the moment, however, politics was not his paramount concern. Mosley was still wealthy (the money he had spent on the British Union, some £2.5 million in today's values, he claimed to have recouped on the stock market). Even so, he, like the rest of the country, had to struggle against the austerity of the final years of war and its aftermath. The nation was exhausted, rationing was strict, and everyday life was hard, even for the rich.

Within weeks of their release, the Mosleys were forced to move on. The government decided that as Professor Jackson was working on 'windows', a top secret device for decoying anti-aircraft fire, Mosley should not be nearby. The Mosleys, their children, faithful Nanny Higgs and a single servant girl, found shelter in the Shaven Crown, a deserted village inn at Shipton-under-Wychwood in the Cotswolds. They were besieged by the press, but since they were forbidden to speak in public, the newspapers got thin pickings. One paparazzo snapped a gaunt and haggard

Mosley carrying a bucket of coal across the yard, an image which delighted his many enemies.

Mosley was sick and depressed. Prison and illness had taken their toll, and he was now prematurely lined and aged, sometimes forced to walk with a stick. Diana shouldered the burden of finding a new home, helped by her friend, the aesthete Lord Berners, one of the few members of her pre-war social set to have remained loyal. Early in 1944, she found what she was looking for at Crux Easton, a rambling old brick house near Newbury. The ultimate plan was for the Mosleys to farm but while they sought a larger property, Diana indulged her passion for interior decoration. Some of their Wootton furniture was brought out of storage and Mosley, his health slowly recovering, began to order his thoughts and write down his vision for the future. Their most immediate problem was the education of their two sons, Alexander and Max. Both boys had been damaged by their enforced separation from their parents, and were wild and uncontrollable. This, coupled with their parents' notoriety, gave several schools a reason to refuse them admission, and the Mosleys settled for a haphazard home education under a changing cast of tutors.

Mosley and Diana with sons Alex and Max

Meanwhile, the war was approaching its end. D-Day came and went, and, hammered on two fronts, Nazi Germany began to collapse. Mosley's prophecies that the war would lead to an expansion of Soviet Communism into the heart of Europe proved correct, and the allied bombing campaign which had reduced many German cities to rubble seemed to bear out his warnings that the war would end with the destruction of European civilisation. While the Mosleys may have drawn a grim satisfaction from this fulfilment of their fears, there is no evidence that they were particularly affected by another consequence of the Allied advance: the discovery of Nazi concentration camps and their emaciated victims.

Early in 1945, the Mosleys bought, sight unseen, since it was outside the seven-mile radius of their home beyond which they were not permitted to travel, a substantial property at Crowood, near Ramsbury in Wiltshire: an 18th-century manor house with 1,100 acres of mixed farmland. When the war in Europe ended with Mussolini's murder, Hitler's suicide and Germany's capitulation in May 1945, the restrictions which had governed Mosley's release were finally removed. Life with his extended family – the children from both his marriages and Diana's children by Bryan Guinness – began at Crowood in a brief summer idyll, marred only by his final estrangement from his sister-in-law Irene, over the guardianship of his son Mickey, who was permanently separated from his father.

While Diana looked after the children and concentrated on home-making at Crowood, Mosley, an old tweed jacket and baggy corduroy trousers replacing his uniforms of the 1930s, managed the farm and began to pick up the threads of his political thought, if not yet his political career. He re-established contact with old fascist friends, and those trying to revive the faith in Germany and elsewhere in Europe. During the course of these contacts he was swindled by one of the era's notorious con men, Gerald Hamilton, the anti-hero of Christopher Isherwood's novel *Mr Norris Changes Trains*. Mosley unwisely entrusted him with a considerable sum which Hamilton promptly spent on himself.

The fruit of Mosley's wartime and post-war thought appeared in

The country life of a farmer occupied Mosley for a time after the war

two books: *My Answer* (1946), a reply to his critics and a restatement of his ideals of combining economic efficiency with dynamic government; and *The Alternative* (1947), a more reflective work in which Mosley sees himself as a philosopher king, informed by his prison reading of Nietzsche, Plato and above all, Goethe's *Faust*. He saw, too late, that the nationalism which fascism had embodied had driven Europe to war and ruin. Henceforth, a narrow British patriotism would have to be subsumed in the ideal of a united Europe. Mosley set himself the task of *learning to think and feel as a European*.[141]

Mosley's transformation from British patriot into European 'post-fascist' also marked a turning point in the history of British fascism, since few of his followers approved, or even understood, his new faith. Lacking Mosley's wealth-fuelled mobility, they remained physically rooted in Britain, and emotionally wedded to their country. Mosley, scorned by the British establishment and rejected by most of his countrymen, no longer felt much loyalty or affection for his native land. Indeed, the final three decades of his life would largely be spent in exile.

Although Mosley shared the technocratic elitism and scorn for democracy of the Europeans who became the founding fathers of today's European Union – politicians such as Robert Schuman, Jean Monnet, Paul Henri Spaak and Alcide de Gasperi – he hardly became a liberal. A key component of his new plans for Europe was that the continent should continue to exploit Africa economically and dominate it politically. Mosley continued to believe in the civilising imperial mission of the white man, and to support apartheid South Africa and the remnants of colonial empire in Africa.

Mosley claimed that his new beliefs represented a synthesis of fascism and democracy. The spread of democracy, he claimed, while bettering the conditions of ordinary people, had smudged out mankind's 'heroic' qualities. He called for a revival of the classical virtues – courage, sacrifice, daring and originality – which the mediocrity and conformity of modern society was eroding. It was surely possible, Mosley reasoned, to reconcile the lucid spirit of the Enlightenment and the pity of Christ with Nietzsche's striving for the superman. Mosley's new motto was Goethe's dictum: 'Only he who continually strives upwards, him can we save.'[142] By adapting Darwin's theory of evolution to political progress, Mosley claimed, modern mankind could build on the disasters of the recent past and beat a new path forward.

Mosley established his own publishing company, Euphorion Books, to get his ideas across. The list was an eclectic compendium including his own books, classics such as Virgil's *Georgics*, a modern novel, translations of Balzac stories by Diana and one surprise bestseller, *Stuka Pilot* – the memoirs of a Nazi Second World War air ace, Hans-Ulrich Rudel. Mosley set up a network of book clubs to distribute the material, and a newsletter commenting on current events. Beneath this cover he was preparing his re-entry into politics.

In November 1947, after the publication of *The Alternative*, he convened a conference of his book clubs at the Farringdon Street Memorial Hall, the site of the ill-starred launch of the New Party 16 years before. In his address, Mosley outlined his vision of a new Europe arising, Phoenix-like, from the ruins of war, and leeching on Africa in *a new system of two continents . . . a civilisation (surpassing) and a force which equalled, any power in the world.*[143]

As Britain shivered through the worst winter in living memory, compounded by the unpopular economic austerity of the Attlee Labour government, elected by a landslide in July 1945, Mosley continued with his plans for a return to the political front line. On 8 February 1948, he launched the Union Movement, campaigning for *Europe a nation*.[144] The programme called for a European government appointed by a European parliament elected by universal European suffrage. In pursuing his goal of opening up Africa as the engine of the new European economy, Mosley endorsed a plan by Oswald Pirow, an Afrikaaner South African ex-Cabinet minister who had been an enthusiastic pro-Nazi during the war, to divide Africa into 'black' and 'white' spheres which would develop in harmony, but at different speeds, reflecting the 'slower' pace of progress in the black two-thirds of the continent.

The problem with Mosley's vision of a post-war future, was, of course, that it rested on the racism of the past. Mosley could not divest himself of the incubus of fascism. This was most evident in the company he chose to keep, the stalwarts of the Union Movement who were familiar faces of the BU and the BUF: Alexander Raven Thomson was its secretary until his death in 1955; and 'Mick' Clarke, the East End rabble-rouser of the 1930s, was another prominent member.

Although Mosley, in the wake of the Holocaust, announced that there was no longer a 'Jewish Question' in British politics, and

The crowds grew smaller at Mosley's rallies, here they assemble in the east London suburb of Dalston 1948

tried to distance his movement from the discredited anti-Semitism of the 1930s, his followers could not be moved from their familiar mindset. The East End soon echoed once more to the sound of battle at Union Movement public meetings held at Railton Road and other locations in Hackney, as Jews and Communists clashed with Mosley's followers. Fuelled by a new burst of anti-Semitism arising from the dirty war between British troops and Zionist guerrillas in Palestine, Mosley's publications were soon replete with the same old anti-Semitic rhetoric.

Mosley himself, now well into his 50s and depressed by the deaths of his mother and Unity in 1948, was not truly in the driving seat of his new movement. Although he occasionally appeared as star speaker at selected meetings, trading insults with hecklers and dodging brickbats as of old, some of the fire had gone out. In keeping with his new European perspective, Mosley announced that he would in future spend more time abroad. Simply getting out of the country, however, proved to be a problem. The Mosleys' passports had been impounded when they were interned, and the authorities refused to issue them with new ones. To get around this, Mosley found a loophole in the law by which British citizens could leave the country without passports providing they found a country willing to admit them. He sought the necessary permission from Spain and Portugal, then still quasi-fascist dictatorships playing host to several old Nazis and fascists from Germany, Italy and France who had managed to escape in 1945. As no airline or shipping line would take the notorious couple, Mosley simply bought his own yacht, the 60-ton *Alianora*, and prepared to depart. At the last moment, the Foreign Office relented and issued new passports. The Mosleys went ahead with their cruise anyway in June 1949, accompanied by Alexander, Max, a crew of two and a butler, and spent the summer and autumn harbour-hopping along the Atlantic seaboard of France, Spain and Portugal, and then through the Mediterranean, renewing old contacts and making new ones.

Enthused by the trip, and wearied by constant battles with the British authorities over tax and other vexations, Mosley decided to make his exile permanent. In 1950, he and Diana left Crowood for Ireland, where they bought Clonfert Palace, a former seat of Anglican bishops, in County Galway. The palace was a dilapidated ruin, but the Mosley family threw themselves into making it habitable.

Ireland had many attractions for them: Diana's sisters Pam and Deborah had houses nearby; and the Dublin authorities took a more relaxed view of taxation – and indeed of fascism – than their British counterparts. Besides, ever since his denunciations of the Black and Tan atrocities at the beginning of his political career, Mosley had always maintained a soft spot for Ireland.

At the same time, having sold Crowood for £80,000 – making a 100 per cent profit in five years – the Mosleys purchased a quirky residence at Orsay, an exclusive suburb near Paris, that became their final and favourite home. The Temple de la Gloire, a Greek-style house of considerable charm, had been built in 1800 as the gift of the French nation to General Moreau, victor over the Prussians at Hohenlinden. The Mosleys fell into an annual round of travel between their various residences (they had also bought a convenient flat in central Paris). Spring was spent in France, while the summer was taken up with vacations in Venice, their pre-war stamping ground. They were in Ireland for the autumn and winter. Their visits to England were now confined, for tax reasons, to 90 days of the year.

The friends they saw varied. In Antibes and Monte Carlo, they partied among the ageing European high society led by the Duke and Duchess of Windsor, near neighbours of the Mosleys in France who became close friends. The two couples had much in common: of a similar age, they had both been lionised and then violently shunned by the British establishment; both had been admirers of Hitler; and both were now almost permanently abroad, with no perceptible purpose in life, living on redundant dreams.

Other friends lacked even the shop-soiled respectability of the Windsors. Mosley followed the tarnished neo-fascist trail around the globe. In Spain, Franco's brother-in-law and sometime Foreign Minister, the pro-Nazi Ramon Serrano Suner, introduced him to Otto Skorzeny, Hitler's commando chief, who had masterminded the successful rescue of Mussolini after the Duce's ousting in 1943. Skorzeny was reputed now to lead the Odessa, the secret organisation protecting former SS members, under his cover as a businessman in Spanish exile. Mosley met other dubious characters when he visited Argentina in November 1950 to inspect the regime of Juan Perón, which had offered a haven to scores of Nazi killers, including Josef Mengele, the butcher of Auschwitz, and Adolf Eichmann, evil genius of the Holocaust. In Italy, the Mosleys' set included aristocrats tainted with fascism, such as

Prince Valerio Borghese, an unreconstructed admirer of Mussolini, known as the 'Black prince', who was still plotting a fascist coup in Italy as late as 1970. Giorgio Almirante, the former Mussolini official who re-built Italian fascism in his MSI (Movimento Soziale Italiano) was another friend. In Germany, Mosley met former SS men, whom, he reported *were passionately European and entirely supported my advanced European ideas.* [145]

Mosley found a more intellectual soulmate in the German writer Ernst Junger, a war hero, who, while articulating the right-wing spirit of the storm troops who had emerged from the trenches, had held aloof from Nazism, and, in his post-1945 book *Der Friede* (*The Peace*) advocated ideas of a new Europe led by an intellectual elite in a new spirit of reconciliation. Such ideas echoed Mosley's *The Alternative*. Junger would survive to be a centenarian, and receive the homage of such European leaders as Helmut Kohl and François Mitterrand as an intellectual godfather of the new Europe.

All these men, respectable new conservatives and criminal old Nazis alike, were articulating a 'third way' between Communism and capitalism that might have won more adherents as well as intellectual credibility had not so many of its advocates been former apostles of fascism or Nazi activists. It would be left to a later European generation to renew such ideas.

Mosley's Last Hurrah

In 1953, attempting to win intellectual credit for his 'new' ideas, Mosley founded a monthly magazine review, *The European*. The editorial work was largely done by Diana and much of the content was by Mosley, with some high-quality literary pieces – mainly by older fascists, including Henry Williamson, Ezra Pound and the South African poet Roy Campbell – and essays by younger neo-fascist intellectuals, chiefly from France. The magazine limped on for six years, but never became the forum Mosley had envisaged for thrashing out a new European ideal.

In 1954, the Mosleys' Irish home, Clonfert Palace, was gutted by fire. They did not have the heart to restore it again, and left it for a smaller home, Ileclash in County Cork. This remained their Irish base until 1963, when it was sold.

Mosley's Union Movement continued doggedly to pursue its path on the streets of London. Personal loyalty to Mosley was now an almost feudal habit among veterans of his movement, who had passed their faith on to their children. Throughout the 1950s and early 1960s, he would make ritual appearances in favoured fascist watering holes in the East End where he raised a pint among adoring acolytes and departed to fascist salutes.

Still banned from the airwaves by the BBC, Mosley also appeared at the Oxford and Cambridge Student Unions, where his still forceful oratory and seemingly rational and 'European' solutions appealed to some in the rising intellectual generation. Now an ageing man, Mosley's appearance had thickened and coarsened.

He still occasionally went through the motions of seduction and infidelity, but more from force of habit than desire.

Mosley's penultimate intervention in British politics came after the Notting Hill race riots of 1958. His Union Movement, despite its official highfalutin European humanism, had been dipping its toes into racism once again. This time, however, the chief target was not the Jews but the new influx of black immigrants from the Caribbean. *Action*, Mosley's revived newspaper, was again abusing 'Hottentots' and 'Fuzzy Wuzzies', and Mosley spoke of 'witch doctors' and 'Ju-ju men'. Although Mosley thought himself a cut above the vulgar British neo-Nazis who had inherited the mantle of Arnold Leese, in practice there was little to distinguish them in the street politics of the gutter.

In August 1958, four days of riots flared in the streets of Notting Hill, the West London area which had become a primary centre of West Indian settlement. Jeffrey Hamm, the Union Movement's Secretary, made a rabble-rousing speech against immigration. Mosley spoke out in defence of the Teddy Boys, the white youth cult of the late 1950s with slicked-back hair, bootlace ties and drainpipe trousers. The Teds had been blamed by the press for leading the anti-black riots, and Mosley was clearly hoping to recruit them to his movement.

The events in Notting Hill marked a serious breach between Mosley and his eldest son, Nicholas. Nicholas had come home from the war as a hero with a Military Cross, and was easily his father's intellectual equal. In prison visits and letters and impassioned discussions after Mosley's release, he had helped hone his father's Faustian ideas, perhaps giving too much credit to the old man's break with the past. Nicholas contributed thoughtful articles to *The European*, but since witnessing the effects of fascism and Nazism first-hand in Italy and Austria, he had not considered himself a fascist. Indeed, he had been pelted by eggs by his half-brother Alexander in April 1958 when he joined the left-

Mosley with Diana and son Max outside the Old Street Court in 1962

wing anti-nuclear bomb march from Aldermaston to London.

Increasingly, Nicholas had been troubled by the mixture of idealism and violence in his father, and saw that just as his father's positive economic ideas between the wars had been discredited by his increasing anti-Semitism, so the 'reasonable' ideas in his postwar political philosophy were being destroyed by anti-black racism.

In the 1959 general election, Mosley stood as Union Movement candidate in North Kensington, which included Notting Hill. Nicholas went along unannounced to one of his father's campaign meetings. 'There was Dad on top of a van again and bellowing; so much older now with his grey hair and grey suit . . . there he was roaring on about such things as black men being able to live on tins of cat food, and teenage girls being kept by gangs of blacks in attics. And there were all the clean-faced young men round his van guarding him; and somewhere, I suppose, the fingers of the devotees of the dark god tearing at him.'[146]

Nicholas confronted his father in Mosley's election office. He found Mosley with Diana and his lawyer. Nervously, Nicholas involuntarily stood to attention like a private on parade and, 'in a frail rage' spewed out the accumulated bile of decades. Mosley, said his son, 'was not only a racialist, but was using racialism to destroy himself.'[147] What he was doing was wrong and squalid. He had done the same before the war, and now, like a dog returning to its vomit, he was repeating the same mistake. Nicholas added that Mosley was a 'rotten father' who had never cared about his children. He had rid himself of responsibility for them as soon as he could, and had shown nothing but contempt when they tried to go their own way. When he had finished this grand, remonstrance, Nicholas stood trembling, almost expecting some thunderbolt to strike him down. Instead, Mosley said quietly: *I will never speak to you again.*[148] The breach between them lasted the best part of the subsequent decade.

On polling day, Mosley scraped 2,821 votes out of 34,912 cast, finishing bottom of the poll. It was an unprecedented humiliation, but still Mosley pressed on. In 1962 he was knocked down while walking to a meeting in Ridley Road. His son Max, who had sprung to his defence, was charged with breach of the peace but acquitted. Mosley attempted to reach a mass audience with meetings in Trafalgar Square, but these were banned after one ended in violence. On several occasions, he recorded television interviews, but they never reached the screen.

In the 1966 general election, now in his 70th year, Mosley fought his last parliamentary campaign when he stood in Shoreditch. Again he came last, scraping together 1,600 votes in his old East End stronghold, a mere 4.6 per cent of the poll. After this, he finally withdrew from British politics to write his memoirs. The Union Movement, still nominally functioning under Jeffrey Hamm, would henceforth have to do without its founder.

An Exiled End

In 1968, Mosley published his autobiography *My Life*, a lengthy apologia that mixed anecdotes and exculpatory ramblings with philosophical digressions and pen portraits of the famous men he had known: David Lloyd George, F D Roosevelt, Winston Churchill and Adolf Hitler. It was unapologetic over his fascism yet almost laughably reticent about his scandalous private life (Diana had edited the opus). Surprisingly, the book received generally glowing reviews. The leftist historian A J P Taylor praised Mosley as 'A superb political thinker',[149] while the sage Malcolm Muggeridge launched a cliché when he said that Mosley was the only man who could have become either or both a Tory and a Labour Prime Minister. The lost leader was indeed the theme of much of the commentary. Mosley won praise for the radical, dynamic solutions he had proposed to deal with the Depression. The book's reception showed, once again, the British trait of heaping praise on a once dangerous figure who has had his claws drawn.

Almost as long as he lived, however, there remained some corner of Mosley which still expected the call of destiny. In interviews throughout the 1960s, he claimed that the long-predicted political and economic crisis would burst upon Britain. When that day came, he said, he still stood ready – just as the ageing Churchill had been in 1940 or Charles de Gaulle in 1958 – to save his country in its hour of need.

Finally, Mosley mellowed. Reconciled with his eldest son via his teenage grandchildren, he held court in France with Diana. Their home was open house to a steady stream of visitors, including bright young university students or society people from Britain, eager for the scent of danger still to be found at the dining table presided over by Mosley with old world courtesy. Mosley was less reluctant than Diana to voice mild criticism of his fascist past. When Hitler was mentioned he closed his eyes and murmured: *Terrible little man.*[150]

Mosley's final years were overshadowed by the onset in 1977 of Parkinson's disease. In November 1980, he was visited by Nicholas, who was surprised by his father's seeming need to unburden himself over an early morning glass of pink champagne. Had he been immoral in his parallel liaison with Baba and Diana in the 1930s, he wondered? Reaching further back, he assured Nicholas that he had enjoyed an ideal life with his mother, Cimmie, just as he did with Diana.

Mosley and Diana in 1977

Nicholas found his father warm, forgiving, humorous and self-mocking. Mosley occasionally collapsed and lay on the floor like a great fallen tree from the effect of the drugs he took to fight his disease. He would shake with laughter at the absurdity of his position. What he wanted above all, he told his eldest son, was reconciliation. Two weeks later, on 2 December, after a day of restless, painful malaise, Oswald Mosley died alone in his bed at Orsay. Diana heard him fall out but reached him too late.

Mosley was cremated at Père-Lachaise cemetery, Paris's city of the dead, in the incongruous company of such fellow non-conformist exiles as Oscar Wilde, Amedeo Modigliani and Jim Morrison. Diana lived on for more than two decades, dying in the summer of 2003, aged 93.

Notes

The works referred to most frequently are abbreviated as follows:

ML Oswald Mosley, *My Life* (Nelson, 1968)
OM Robert Skidelsky, *Oswald Mosley* (Macmillan, 1975)
RG Nicholas Mosley, *Rules of the Game* (Secker & Warburg, 1977)
BP Nicholas Mosley, *Beyond the Pale* (Secker & Warburg, 1983)
D Harold Nicolson, *Diaries*, ed Nigel Nicolson (Collins, 1961)

1. *ML*
2. *ML*
3. *OM*
4. Personal interview with author
5. Sigmund Freud, *Four Lectures on Psycho-Analysis* (Penguin)
6. *ML*
7. *ML*
8. *OM*
9. *ML*
10. *ML*
11. *ML*
12. *ML*
13. Alan Clark, *Aces High* (Cassell, 1999)
14. *ML*
15. *ML*
16. *ML*
17. *ML*
18. *ML*
19. *OM*
20. *OM*
21. Quoted in Nicholas Comfort, *Brewer's Politics: A Phrase and Fable Dictionary* (Cassell, 1995)
22. *OM*
23. Anne de Courcy, *The Viceroy's Daughters* (Weidenfeld & Nicolson, 2000)
24. *The Viceroy's Daughters*
25. *RG*
26. *ML*
27. 'Parliamentary Debates', House of Commons (20 October 1920)
28. 'Parliamentary Debates',

House of Commons (24 November 1920)
29 'Parliamentary Debates', House of Commons (5 March 1921)
30 *RG*
31 Beatrice Webb, *The Diaries of Beatrice Webb*, ed Norman and Jeanne Mackenzie (Virago, 2000)
32 *OM*
33 Frederick, Second Earl of Birkenhead, *F.E. Smith* (Eyre & Spottiswoode, 1959)
34 *OM*
35 *OM*
36 'Parliamentary Debates', House of Commons (18 January 1924)
37 *OM*
38 *OM*
39 Egon Wertheimer, 'Portrait of the Labour Party' (1929)
40 'Portrait of the Labour Party'
41 *OM*
42 *OM*
43 John Strachey, 'Revolution by Reason' (1925)
44 'Revolution by Reason'
45 *OM*
46 *Westminster Gazette* (17 December 1926)
47 *Daily Mail* (16 December 1926)
48 *Daily Express* (13 December 1926)
49 *OM*
50 *Birmingham Post* (23 December 1926)
51 *The Diaries of Beatrice Webb*
52 *RG*
53 *OM*
54 *The Viceroy's Daughters*
55 *The Diaries of Beatrice Webb*
56 Oswald Mosley, 'The Greater Britain' (ed. 1934)
57 *OM*
58 *RG*
59 *OM*
60 *RG*
61 *The Times* (27 May 1930)
62 *Sunday Express* (30 May 1930)
63 *OM*
64 *OM*
65 *Punch* (17 December 1930)
66 *Observer* (7 December 1930)
67 *ML*
68 *OM*
70 *OM*
71 John Strachey, 'The Menace of Fascism' (1933)
72 'The Menace of Fascism'
73 *RG*
74 *OM*
75 *OM*
76 'Parliamentary Debates', House of Commons (8 September 1924)
77 *OM*
78 *D*
79 *Action* (31 December 1931)
80 *Action*
81 Friedrich Nietzsche, *Thus*

Spake Zarathustra from *Gesammalte Werke* tr Oscar Levy (T N Foulis, 1909–13)

82 John Woodhouse, *Gabriele D'Annunzio: Defiant Archangel* (Oxford University Press, 1998)

83 *The Viceroy's Daughters*

84 *D*

85 *Daily Mail* (1 February 1932)

86 *D*

87 *OM*

88 'The Greater Britain'

89 'The Greater Britain'

90 *OM*

91 Diana Mosley, *A Life of Contrasts* (Hamish Hamilton, 1977)

92 *A Life of Contrasts*

93 Robert Boothby, 'I Fight to Live' (1947)

94 *The Viceroy's Daughters*

95 *D*

96 *RG*

97 *The Viceroy's Daughters*

98 *The Viceroy's Daughters*

99 *The Viceroy's Daughters*

100 Kenneth Young, *Stanley Baldwin* (Weidenfeld & Nicolson, 1976)

101 *Stanley Baldwin*

102 Julie Gottlieb, *Feminine Fascism* (I B Tauris, 2000)

103 *BP*

104 *BP*

105 Eye-witness accounts of Olympia – all hostile to Mosley – appear in *Fascists at Olympia* compiled by 'Vindicator' (Gollancz, 1934); and Frederic Mullally, *Fascism Inside England* (Claud Morris Books, 1946). I am grateful to Mr Mullally for recalling Olympia and other fascist meetings that he witnessed in a personal interview. There are accounts by Special Branch informants in the National Archives (MEPOL 2/4319). The BUF published their own defence in *Red Violence and Blue Lies*. (1934)

106 *The Times* (8 June 1934)

107 *The Times* (9 June 1934)

108 *Sunday Pictorial* (24 June 1934)

109 Private letter from Lloyd George in the Mosley papers

110 *The Blackshirt* (1934)

111 Francis Beckett, *The Rebel Who Lost His Cause: the Tragedy of John Beckett MP* (London House, 1999)

112 Josef Goebbels, *Tagebucher* (Saur, 1987-2000)

113 *ML*

114 *Tagebucher*

115 Anthony John Trythall, *'Boney' Fuller: The Intellectual General* (Cassell, 1977)

116 A K Chesterton, 'Why I Left Mosley' (1938)
117 *BP*
118 *ML*
119 Douglas Hyde, *I Believed: The Autobiography of a Former British Communist* (Reprint Society, 1951)
120 *BP*. For a recent eye-witness account of Mosley at Cable Street, see *Brief Lives* by W F 'Bill' Deedes (2004).
121 *OM*
122 Piers Brendon, *The Dark Valley: A Panorama of the 1930s* (Cape, 2000)
123 *The Rebel Who Lost His Cause: The Tragedy of John Beckett MP*
124 *OM*
125 *BP*
126 *The Rebel Who Lost His Cause*
127 *BP*
128 *The Rebel Who Lost His Cause*
129 *Why I Left Mosley*
130 P G Wodehouse, *The Code of the Woosters* (Vintage, 1990)
131 Oswald Mosley, *Tomorrow We Live* (BUF, 1938)
132 *BP*
133 *ML*
134 *A Life of Contrasts*
135 *OM*
136 *ML*
137 *ML*
138 'Parliamentary Debates', House of Commons (17 November 1943)
139 *Daily Worker* (18 November 1943)
140 Charles-Maurice de Talleyrand, *Oxford Dictionary of Quotations* (1953)
141 *ML*
142 Johann Wolfgang von Goethe, *Faust*
143 *OM*
144 *OM*
145 *ML*
146 *BP*
147 *BP*
148 *BP*
149 *Observer* (nd)
150 Nicholas Mosley to author

Chronology

Year	Age	Life
1896		16 November: In London, Oswald Ernald Mosley born.
1905	8	Enters West Downs preparatory school, Winchester, Hampshire.
1909	12	Enters Winchester College.
1914	17	January: Accepted by the Royal Military Academy, Sandhurst, but is sent down following a brawl. August: Recalled and commissioned into 16th Lancers. Trains at the Curragh, Ireland before being transferred to the Royal Flying Corps.
1915	18	Based at Bailleul, near Ypres, France. April: Flies as an observer of second Battle of Ypres. Qualifies as pilot. In the area around Loos, serves in trenches.
1916	19	Invalided back to Britain with leg injuries. Begins series of desk jobs in War Ministries at Whitehall.
1917	20	Introduced to political salons of London.

Year	History	Culture
1896	Theodore Herzl founds Zionism. First Olympic Games of the modern era held in Athens.	Giacomo Puccini, *La Bohème*. Thomas Hardy, *Jude the Obscure*.
1905	Bloody Sunday massacre. Korea becomes protectorate of Japan.	Richard Strauss, *Salome*. Paul Cézanne, *Les Grandes Baigneuses*.
1909	In Britain, Lloyd George's 'People's Budget' is rejected by House of Lords; causes constitutional crisis. In Turkey, Young Turk revolution. Henry Ford introduces Model T car.	Strauss, *Elektra*. Rabindranath Tagore, *Gitanjali*. Sergey Diaghilev forms Les Ballets Russes. E F T Marinetti publishes manifesto of futurism in *Le Figaro*.
1914	28 June: Archduke Franz Ferdinand assassinated in Sarajevo; First World War begins. Panama Canal opens. Egypt becomes British protectorate.	James Joyce, *Dubliners*. Ezra Pound, *Des Imagistes*.
1915	Dardanelles/Gallipoli campaign (until 1916). In Brussels, Germans execute Edith Cavell. Albert Einstein introduces general theory of relativity.	John Buchan, *The Thirty-Nine Steps*. D H Lawrence, *The Rainbow*. Ezra Pound, *Cathay*. Pablo Picasso, *Harlequin*.
1916	Battle of the Somme. Battle of Jutland. Easter Rising in Ireland. Arabs revolt against Ottoman Turks.	Guillaume Apollinaire, *Le poète assassiné*. G B Shaw, *Pygmalion*. Dada movement launched in Zurich with Cabaret Voltaire.
1917	US enters First World War. British take Baghdad. Balfour Declaration on Palestine: Britain favours creation of Jewish state.	First recording of New Orleans jazz. Franz Kafka, *Metamorphosis*. T S Eliot, *Prufrock and Other Observations*.

Year	Age	Life
1918	22	December: In Harrow, elected for the Conservative Party; youngest MP in House of Commons.
1920	23	Marries Lady Cynthia Curzon at Chapel Royal, London.
1921	24	Speaks out against government repression in Ireland. November: Crosses floor of Commons to sit as Independent MP. Birth of Vivien, first child.
1922	26	November: Returned as Independent MP.
1923	26	Birth of Nicholas, first son.
1924	27	March: Joins Labour Party. October: In Birmingham Ladywood, loses election. December: Visits India.
1925	28	With John Strachey, writes 'Revolution by Reason', a Keynesian economic tract.
1926	29/30	May: Visits US and meets F D Roosevelt. December: In Birmingham Smethwick, wins by-election.
1928	31	Visits central Europe with Ramsay MacDonald.
1929	32	May: Appointed Chancellor of the Duchy of Lancaster (minister without portfolio). Charged with combating unemployment.
1930	33	May: Resigns from government.

Year	History	Culture
1918	11 November: Armistice agreement ends First World War. In UK, women over 30 get right to vote. Food shortage leads to establishment of National Food Kitchens and rationing; Prime Minister appeals to women to help with the harvest.	Oswald Spengler, *The Decline of the West*, Volume 1. Amédée Ozenfant and Le Corbusier, *Après le Cubisme*. Paul Klee, *Gartenplan*. *Tarzan of the Apes* with Elmo Lincoln.
1920	IRA formed.	Edith Wharton, *The Age of Innocence*.
1921	Paris conference of wartime Allies fixes Germany's reparation payments: Rhineland occupied. National Economic Policy in Soviet Union.	Sergei Prokofiev, *The Love of Three Oranges*. Luigi Pirandello, *Six Characters in Search of an Author*. Chaplin, *The Kid*.
1922	Soviet Union formed. Benito Mussolini's fascists march on Rome.	T S Eliot, *The Waste Land*. Joyce, *Ulysses*.
1923	End of the Ottoman empire.	Le Corbusier, *Vers une architecture*.
1924	Vladimir Lenin dies.	Forster, *A Passage to India*. Thomas Mann, *The Magic Mountain*. André Breton, first surrealist manifesto.
1925	Chiang Kai-shek launches campaign to unify China. Discovery of ionosphere.	F Scott Fitzgerald, *The Great Gatsby*. Kafka, *The Trial*.
1926	Germany joins League of Nations. Hirohito becomes emperor of Japan.	Hemingway, *The Sun Also Rises*. A A Milne, *Winnie the Pooh*. Fritz Lang, *Metropolis*.
1928	Kellogg-Briand Pact for Peace. Alexander Fleming discovers penicillin.	Maurice Ravel, *Boléro*. Kurt Weill, *The Threepenny Opera*. D H Lawrence, *Lady Chatterley's Lover*. Walt Disney, *Steamboat Willie*.
1929	Wall Street Crash. Young Plan for Germany.	Ernest Hemingway, *A Farewell to Arms*. Erich Maria Remarque, *All Quiet on the Western Front*.
1930	Mahatma Gandhi leads Salt March in India. Frank Whittle patents turbo-jet engine. Pluto discovered.	W H Auden, *Poems*. T S Eliot, 'Ash Wednesday'. William Faulkner, *As I Lay Dying*. Evelyn Waugh, *Vile Bodies*.

Year	Age	Life
1931	34/35	January: Receives funding from William Morris, car tycoon, to create a new political party. March: Formally expelled from Labour Party. October: In Stoke, Cynthia's seat, loses election. December: New Party is folded.
1932	35	January: Visits Rome. Publicly expresses admiration for Benito Mussolini's fascist regime. Writes 'The Greater Britain', a fascist manifesto. April: Birth of Mickey, second son. June: Meets Diana Guinness; they become lovers. October: Forms British Union of Fascists (BUF). First public meeting in Trafalgar Square.
1933	36	April: Second visit to Rome. In fascist uniform, reviews parade alongside Mussolini. May: Cynthia dies.
1934	37	January: Lord Rothermere, head of Harmsworth Press, which includes the *Daily Mail*, provides support to Mosley's blackshirts. June: At Olympia, London, BUF holds mass rally that is broken up by violence. July: Lord Rothermere withdraws support for BUF.
1935	38	April: In Munich, has private meeting with Adolf Hitler.
1936	39	March: At the Royal Albert Hall, London, BUF holds mass rally. June: Mosley renames BUF the British Union of Fascists and National Socialists (BU) and introduces an SS-style uniform for party leadership. October: In Berlin, Mosley marries Diana Guinness at ceremony hosted by Joseph Goebbels and attended by Hitler.
1937	40	March: In London County Council elections, BU fails to make any headway. Mosley purges party leadership. Alexander, first child with Diana, is born.
1938	41	Mosley writes 'Tomorrow we Live' in which he proclaims himself a National Socialist.
1939	42	July: At Earl's Court, London, BU holds mass rally.

Year	History	Culture
1931	King Alfonso XIII flees; Spanish Republic formed. Japan occupies Manchuria. Empire State Building completed.	Rakhmaninov's music banned in the USSR as 'decadent'. St-Exupéry, *Vol de nuit*. *City Lights* (starring Charlie Chaplin)
1932	Kingdom of Saudi Arabia and Kingdom of Iraq become independent. James Chadwick discovers neutron. First autobahn opened, between Cologne and Bonn.	Aldous Huxley, *Brave New World*. Jules Romains, *Les hommes de bonne volonté*. Bertolt Brecht, *The Mother*. Thomas Beecham founds London Philharmonic Orchestra.
1933	Adolf Hitler appointed German chancellor. F D Roosevelt President in US; launches New Deal.	André Malraux, *La condition humaine*. Gertrude Stein, *The Autobiography of Alice B Toklas*.
1934	In China, Mao Tse-tung starts on the Long March. Enrico Fermi sets off first controlled nuclear reaction.	Shostakovich, *Lady Macbeth of Mtsensk*. Agatha Christie, *Murder on the Orient Express*. Henry Miller, *Tropic of Cancer*.
1935	In Germany, Nuremberg Laws enacted. Philippines becomes self-governing. Italy invades Ethiopia.	George Gershwin, *Porgy and Bess*. Marx Brothers, *A Night at the Opera*.
1936	Germany occupies Rhineland. Edward VIII abdicates throne in Britain; George VI becomes King. Spanish Civil War (until 1939).	Prokofiev, *Peter and the Wolf*. A J Ayer, *Language, Truth and Logic*. BBC public television founded.
1937	Japan invades China: Nanjing massacre. Arab-Jewish conflict in Palestine.	Jean-Paul Sartre, *La Nausée*. John Steinbeck, *Of Mice and Men*. Picasso, *Guernica*.
1938	Kristallnacht: in Germany, Jewish buildings are burnt down and shops looted. Austrian Anschluss with Germany.	Elizabeth Bowen, *The Death of the Heart*. Graham Greene, *Brighton Rock*. Evelyn Waugh, *Scoop*. Sergei Eisenstein, *Alexander Nevsky*.
1939	1 September: Germany invades Poland. Francisco Franco becomes dictator of Spain. Britain and France declare war on Germany.	Steinbeck, *The Grapes of Wrath*. John Ford, *Stagecoach* (starring John Wayne). David O Selznick, *Gone with the Wind* (starring Vivien Leigh and Clark Gable)

Year	Age	Life
1940	43/44	May: Max, second child with Diana, is born. Mosley interned in Brixton prison. June: Diana Mosley interned in Holloway prison. July: BU is formally banned. December: Mosley permitted to make monthly visits to Diana.
1941	44	November: Mosley permitted to join in Diana in Holloway.
1943	47	November: Mosley and Diana released from prison on grounds of deteriorating health.
1946	49	Publishes 'My Answer', a rebuttal of his critics.
1947	50	Publishes 'The Alternative', a vision for a post-fascist Europe that rejects nationalism.
1948	51	February: Launches Union Movement (UM).
1949	52	June: Leaves Britain on yacht trip around Mediterranean. In Spain and Italy, renews contact with other European fascists.
1950	53/54	Settles in Ireland. Purchases Temple de la Gloire at Orsay, near Paris. November: Visits Argentina; meets Juan Perón and old Nazis given shelter there.
1953	56	Lanches *The European*.
1958	61	August: Notting Hill race riots. Union Movement stokes anti-black immigration prejudices and woos 'Teddy Boys'.

Year	History	Culture
1940	Germany occupies France, Belgium, the Netherlands, Norway and Denmark. In UK, Churchill becomes PM. Leon Trotsky assassinated in Mexico.	Graham Greene, *The Power and the Glory*. Ernest Hemingway, *For Whom the Bell Tolls*. Chaplin, *The Great Dictator.* Disney, *Fantasia*.
1941	Germany invades Soviet Union. Japan attacks Pearl Harbour: US enters Second World War.	Bertolt Brecht, *Mother Courage and her Children*. Orson Welles, *Citizen Kane*.
1943	Allies bomb Germany and invade Italy: Mussolini deposed.	Rodgers and Hammerstein, *Oklahoma*. Sartre, *Being and Nothingness*. T S Eliot, *Four Quartets*.
1946	In Argentina, Juan Perón becomes president. In Britain, National Health Service founded. Winston Churchill makes 'Iron Curtain' speech.	Bertrand Russell, *History of Western Philosophy*. Sartre, *Existentialism and Humanism*. Eugene O'Neill, *The Iceman Cometh*. Jean Cocteau, *La Belle et la Bête*.
1947	Truman Doctrine. India becomes independent. Chuck Yeager breaks the sounds barrier.	Tennessee Williams, *A Streetcar Named Desire*. Albert Camus, *The Plague*. Anne Frank, *The Diary of Anne Frank*.
1948	Marshall Plan (until 1951). Soviet blockade of Western sectors of Berlin: US and Britain organise airlift. In South Africa, apartheid legislation passed. Gandhi is assassinated. State of Israel founded.	Brecht, *The Caucasian Chalk Circle*. Greene, *The Heart of the Matter*. Norman Mailer, *The Naked and the Dead*. Alan Paton, *Cry, the Beloved Country*. Vittorio De Sica, *Bicycle Thieves*.
1949	NATO formed. Republic of Ireland formed. Mao proclaims China a People's Republic.	George Orwell, *1984*. Simone de Beauvoir, *The Second Sex*. Arthur Miller, *Death of a Salesman*.
1950	Schuman Plan. Korean War begins. China conquers Tibet. In US, McCarthyism starts.	Billy Wilder, *Sunset Boulevard*.
1953	Stalin dies. Korean War ends. Francis Crick and James Watson discover double helix (DNA).	Dylan Thomas, *Under Milk Wood*. Arthur Miller, *The Crucible*. Federico Fellini, *I Vitelloni*.
1958	Fifth French Republic; Charles de Gaulle becomes president. Castro leads Communist revolution in Cuba.	Boris Pasternak, *Dr Zhivago*. Claude Lévi-Strauss, *Structural Anthropology*. Harold Pinter, *The Birthday Party*.

Year	Age	Life
1959	62	In North Kensington, defeated in general election as UM candidate.
1962	65	Attends Venice Summit, meeting of extreme-right European leaders which calls for a united Europe.
1966	69	March: In Shoreditch, defeated in general election as UM candidate. Retires from active politics.
1968	71	Publishes *My Life*, autobiography.
1980	84	3 December: In Paris, dies.

Year	History	Culture
1959	In US, Alaska and Hawaii are admitted to the Union. Solomon Bandaranaike, PM of Ceylon (Sri Lanka), is assassinated.	Motown Records founded. Buddy Holly dies in plane crash. *Ben Hur* (directed by William Wyler). Günter Grass, *The Tin Drum*.
1962	Cuban missile crisis. Jamaica, Trinidad and Tobago, and Uganda become independent.	Edward Albee, *Who's Afraid of Virginia Woolf?* David Lean, *Lawrence of Arabia*.
1966	France ends boycott of EEC meeting and withdraws from NATO. Ian Smith declares Rhodesia a republic.	Graham Greene, *The Comedians*. Sylvia Plath, *Ariel*. Stravinsky, *Requiem Canticles*.
1968	Tet Offensive. In US, M L King and Robert Kennedy assassinated. In Paris, student riots.	Kubrick, *2001: A Space Odyssey*. The Rolling Stones, *Beggar's Banquet*.
1980	Rhodesia independent (Zimbabwe). President Tito of Yugoslavia dies. Polish strikers occupy Lenin shipyard in Gdansk. In US, Reagan elected President.	Michael Jackson, *Thriller*. Richard Attenborough, *Gandhi*. Werner Herzog, *Fitzcarraldo*. Spielberg, *ET*

Further Reading

Remarkably, there is as yet no satisfactory full-length biography of the leader of British fascism. *Oswald Mosley* (1975) by the political economist and academic Robert Skidelsky was published during its subject's lifetime with Mosley's co-operation and, presumably, his approval. It is an exhaustive work and contains much valuable information and interesting discussions of Mosley's philosophy, his economic nostrums and such contentious issues as anti-Semitism and violence. However, it is uninformative about Mosley's personal life generally and it leans over backwards to be fair to Mosley, controversially acquitting him of responsibility for fascism's grosser aspects. It is, in short, broadly pro-Mosley and its author seems now – to judge by recent comments – to rather regret that. Skidelsky's book badly needs updating: since it was written, a mass of new information has emerged about, for example, the foreign financing of the BUF, and the role of MI5 in its affairs, as well as much academic analysis of fascism. All this should be incorporated in Stephen Dorrill's forthcoming and long-awaited biography of Mosley, which promises to be as anti-Mosley as Skidelsky was sympathetic. Mosley's own autobiography, *My Life* (1968) is tendentious, self-serving and aggressively defensive on the many controversies of his career.

By far the most interesting, reflective and revealing books about Mosley are those written by his eldest son Nicholas just before and soon after his father's death. Despite their differences, Mosley left his papers to Nicholas, who used them to produce two classic books, perhaps the most remarkable volumes written by a son about his father. *Rules of the Game* (1977) covers Mosley's marriage with Cimmie and his early political career, while *Beyond the Pale* (1983) continues the story through fascism, Diana, the war, and Mosley's post-war career. Together they represent a heroic attempt by a son to come to terms with a father he despised and loved by turns, yet came, in the end, to understand and forgive. Diana regarded these volumes as an unforgivable betrayal, and they led to a final breach with her stepson.

Mosley's wives have been much better served by biographers. The lives of Cimmie and her sisters, Baba and Irene, have been fascinatingly chronicled by Anne De Courcy in *The Viceroy's Daughters* (2000). The same author has recently given us a gossipy life of *Diana Mosley* (2003) published only after Diana's death. Diana's career had previously been recorded by Jan Dalley in *Diana Mosley: A Life* (1999), which some saw as overly sympathetic to its subject, while the lives of the Mitfords are the subject of *The Mitford Sisters* by Mary Lovell (2001). The extraordinary story of Unity Mitford is told in *Unity: A Quest* (1977) by David Pryce-Jones. Diana also wrote an autobiography, *A Life of Contrasts* (1977, updated [2002] just before her death in August 2003), which holds back from real revelation, hiding bitterness behind a kind of brittle gaiety.

British fascism has become an academic growth industry in recent years, and there are many excellent studies of the subject. Some essential works indispensable to both the student and the general reader include: Colin Cross's *The Fascists in Britain* (1961), the first history of Mosley's movement by a critical, but reasonably objective journalist, and Robert Benewick's *The Fascist Movement in Britain* (1972), which is dated but recommended. *Fascism in Britain* by Richard Thurlow (1987) is the best comprehensive analytical history of the subject. The same author coedited *British Fascism* (1980), a collection of essays which includes Robert Skidelsky's revised views on Mosley.

Richard Griffiths's *Fellow Travellers of the Right* (1983) sheds light on the worryingly widespread British Hitler fan club, who were by no means all fascists. His sequel, *Patriotism Perverted* (1998), focuses on Archibald Maule Ramsay, MP's Right Club and its treasonable activities in 1939–40, and is a useful insight into the background to internment.

On anti-Semitism, Colin Holmes's *Anti-Semitism in British Society 1876–1939* (1979) is definitive. The same author's forthcoming biography of William Joyce is eagerly awaited. Thomas P Linehan's *East London for Mosley* (1996) is a specialised study of Mosley's enduring support in the East End while Trevor Grundy's *Memories of a Fascist Childhood* (1998) is an interesting memoir of a family of East End Mosley loyalists from the 1930s to the 1950s. *Feminine Fascism* by Julie Gottlieb (2000) is ground-breaking and revealing on the vital role of women in Mosley's movement, while Brian Simpson's *In the Highest Degree Odious* (1992) is an in-depth study of wartime internment.

Studies of British fascist leaders other than Mosley are thin on the ground, although a clutch of William Joyce biographies has recently appeared, notably by Mary Kenny (2004). We also have J A Cole's *Lord Haw-Haw* (1987); and David Baker's *Ideology of Obsession* (1996) on A K Chesterton. Graham Macklin is working on an account that carries Chesterton's career beyond 1945. Perhaps most interesting in this field is Francis Beckett's biography of his father John Beckett, *The Rebel Who Lost His Cause* (1999), as objective in its own way as Nicholas Mosley's work on his father.

Fictional accounts of Mosley's fascism include the later books in Henry Williamson's 15-volume sequence of autobiographical novels, *A Chronicle of Ancient Sunlight* (1951–69). These are hero-worshipping works by a true believer and their fulsome adulation even embarrassed their subject – *Henry will take it all so seriously*, Mosley is reputed to have murmured. A recent antidote is Guy Walters' *The Leader* (2003) a Buchanesque thriller which portrays a Mosley-run Britain with chilling credibility.

Acknowledgements

I am grateful, as always, to my indefatigable agent, Andrew Lownie, who, knowing of my interest in Mosley, put me in touch with my publisher Barbara Schwepcke, whose patience in awaiting a long-overdue book has been exemplary. I hope it has been worth it.

Nicholas Mosley heads the list of those authors who knew or have written on Oswald Mosley and have shared their knowledge and insights with me. These include Lord Robert Skidelsky, Frederic Mullaly, David Pryce-Jones, and my friends Hugh Purcell, Francis Beckett and Desmond Seward. My warmest thanks to them all, and to my rigorous editor at Haus, Ravi Mattu.

My partner Lally Freeborn has shared her life with Mosley for longer than either of us had bargained for. To her, as ever, my love.

Picture Sources

The author and the publishers wish to express their thanks to the following sources of illustrative material and/or permission to reproduce it. They will make proper acknowledgements in future editions in the event that any omissions have occurred.

Getty Images: pp. i, iii, 8, 19, 20, 24, 34, 36, 39, 43,47, 59, 64, 75, 97, 99, 105, 110, 113, 115, 124, 126, 129, 131, 134, 141, 145; HIP: pp. 1; Imperial War Museum: pp. 11, 79; Mirrorpix: pp. 102, 143, 148, 154; Topham Picturepoint: pp. 2, 15, 21, 25, 29, 30, 45, 57, 69, 81, 84, 86, 90, 120, 157.

Index

16th Lancers, 10, 13

Abyssinia, 52, 103
Action, 62, 64, 65, 70; revived under BUF and BU, 95, 123, 124, 131; revived again, 153
Aeroplane, The, 87
Africa, 146–7
Air Time, 125
Albania, 52
Aldermaston march, 154
Aldershot, 9
Alexander, A V, 58
Allen, W E D ('Bill'), 57, 83, 96, 117
Almirante, Giorgio, 151
American War of Independence, 139
Amritsar massacre, 24
Anglo-German Fellowship, 126
Anstruther-Grey, W J, 92
Antibes, 42, 46, 62, 150
anti-Semitism, 71, 94, 101, 114, 123, 131; Mosley's, 51, 78–9, 99–100, 102, 113, 123, 138, 154; Mosley tries to renounce, 148
Apeforth, Staffordshire, 4
Argentina, 150
Arlen, Michael, 62
Ascot, 139
Ashton-under-Lyme, 58–9
Asquith, H H, 18, 25, 27, 29, 31
Aston, 35, 44
Astor, Nancy, 20
Attlee, Clement, 80, 84, 147
Austria, 43, 68, 153; Anschluss, 128
Avignon, 76

Bailey, Jim, 124
Bailleul, 11, 13
Baldwin, Oliver, 54–6
Baldwin, Stanley, 18, 30, 44, 52, 128; in National Government, 61, 63; distrust of Mosley, 88; and abdication crisis, 119–21
Balzac, Honoré de, 146
Banbury, 134
Battle of Britain, 136
Bayreuth, 130
BBC, 54, 61, 65, 80, 98, 101, 152
Beamish, Henry Hamilton, 71
Beaton, Cecil, 41, 62
Beaumont, M W, 92
Beaverbrook, Lord, 57, 120
Beckett, John, 84–5, 113, 120–1; sacked from BU, 122–3; accusation against Lord Camrose, 124; interned, 135
Belgium, 99
Belloc, Hilaire, 25
Belton Hall, 6
Berlin, 41, 116, 117, 127; Olympics, 105, 108
Berlin Philharmonic Orchestra, 135
Berners, Lord, 143
Bevan, Aneurin, 51, 54; warns Mosley against fascism, 55
Bevin, Ernest, 54
Birkett, Norman, 138
Birmingham, 34, 35, 38–9, 43, 45, 54, 85
Birmingham Post, 40
Black and Tans, 25, 149
Blackshirt, The, 94, 95, 98, 123
'Blackshirt' cigarettes, 98
Blackshirt Defence Squad, 95
Blackshirts, 58, 80, 85–8, 91–3, 111, 112, 114
Bloody Sunday massacre, 25
Boer War, 139
Bonar Law, Andrew, 21, 28, 30
Boothby, Bob, 37, 41, 42, 49–51; supports 'Mosley Manifesto', 54; and Mosley's infidelities, 76–7; warns Mosley against fascism, 79; visits Mosley in prison, 137

INDEX 177

Borghese, Prince Valerio, 151
Box, F M, 96
Bracken, Brendan, 41, 76
Britain (England): abdication crisis, 119–21; anti-Semitism, 100–1; broadcasting, 98–9; Communists, 95; economy, 62–5, 70; fascism, 59, 67, 69–70, 88, 90–1, 110, 118, 145; 'Jewish Question', 147; post-Second World War, 34; public opinion, 128–9, 134; social change, 14
British Empire, 17, 61, 89, 107, 127, 139, 146
British Fascists (BF), 72–3
British People's Party, 135
British Union of Fascists (BUF), 68, 73, 77–8, 83–98, 101–4, 112–13, 147; 'The Black House', 85, 93, 96, 111; membership, 86–8, 96, 104, 109; Olympia rally, 90–3, 98, 101–2; draws attention of secret services, 93; funding, 95–8, 108, 113; anti-Semitism, 101; decline, 101–2, 109, 111; history, 109; SS-style uniform, 113; changed of name, 113; *see also* British Union of Fascists and National Socialists
British Union of Fascists and National Socialists (British Union or BU), 113–14, 118–24, 147; membership, 118, 128; uniform, 119; 'Stand by the King' campaign, 121; London County Council elections, 121–2; purge, 122–3; funding, 122, 132, 138, 142; lampooned by Nancy Mitford, 126–7; 'Peace Campaign', 128–9; declaration of loyalty, 131; penetrated by security services, 132; staff interned, 133, 136, 138; formally banned, 133; Mosley defends under interrogation, 138–9
Britons Society, 100
Brittain, Vera, 91
Brockway, Fenner, 53
Brown, Ivor, 90
Brown, W J, 54–6
Brunswick, Princess of, 107–8
Buckinghamshire, 40
bull-baiting, 6

Cambridge University, 28; Union, 80, 152
Campbell, J R, 34
Campbell, Roy, 152
Campbell, Sir Malcolm, 87
Camrose, Lord, 124
Cecil, Lord Robert, 23, 27, 29; biography, 24
Chamberlain, Houston Stewart, 67
Chamberlain, Neville, 34, 53, 128, 130, 132
Chamberlayne, A R, 17
Charles I, King, 2
Charles II, King, 3
Chatham, Lord, 139
Chesterton, A K, 84, 101, 111, 113; sacked from BU, 124; joins forces, 131

Chesterton, G K, 25, 84
Cheyney, Peter, 65
Churchill, Clementine, 140
Churchill, Randolph, 76
Churchill, Winston, 15, 18, 57, 75; approaches to Mosley, 61, 70, 79; excluded from National Government, 63; friends associated with BUF, 87; distrust of Mosley, 88; and 'King's party' idea, 120; becomes Prime Minister, 132; promotes US intervention in war, 132–3; and Mosleys' internment, 136–41; described in *My Life*, 156
Clark, Alan, 11
Clarke, 'Mick', 112, 114, 121, 147
Clayton, C F, 136
Cliveden, 81, 85
Clonfert Palace, 149, 152
Cobden, Richard, 3
Cole, G D H, 25
Colefax, Lady Sybil, 26, 61
Collins, Michael, 25
Common, Jack 'Spot', 115
Communism, 39, 55, 78, 151; Soviet, 65, 143
Communist Party, 90–1, 109, 112
Communists, 58, 65, 109, 114; fighting fascists, 64, 84, 112, 116, 138, 148; at Olympia, 91, 93; in Spanish Civil War, 126; supported by Moscow, 95
Comte, Auguste, 67
concentration camps, 144
Conservatives, *see* Tories
Contrexville, 77
Cook, Arthur, 42, 54
Corn Laws, 3
County Cork, 152
County Galway, 149
Courtaulds, 98
Coward, Noël, 62
Crisis, 121
Cromwell, Oliver, 3, 71
Crowood, 144, 149
Crux Easton, 143
Cunard, Lady Blanche, 15, 26
Curragh, the, 10
Curzon, George Nathaniel, Viscount, 19–21, 30, 33; biography, 19; breach with Cimmie, 26; death, 26
Curzon, Lady Alexandra (Baba), *see* Metcalfe, Baba
Curzon, Lady Cynthia (Cimmie), *see* Mosley, Lady Cynthia (Cimmie)
Curzon, Lady Irene, 20, 46, 79, 81, 89; guardian of Mosley's children, 134, 144
Czechoslovakia, 43, 128

d'Annunzio, Gabriele, 67
D'Erlanger, Catherine, 15
Daily Express, 40, 58

178 INDEX

Daily Herald, 60, 140
Daily Mail, 4, 33, 40, 68, 70, 88, 98
Daily Telegraph, 124
Daily Worker, 91, 141
Dalton, Hugh, 32, 39
Dante Alighieri, 23
Darwin, Charles, 146
Davies, Sellick, 63
Davison, John, 39
Dawson of Penn, Lord, 140
De Gasperi, Alcide, 146
de Gaulle, Charles, 156
Defence Regulation 18(b), 132–3
Denham, Buckinghamshire, 43, 80, 131, 133; home to Mosley's children, 40, 85, 89, 112, 125; Ramsay MacDonald visits, 47, 50; New Party leadership gather at, 60; Cimmie buried in, 81; requisitioned, 134
Denmark, 99
Depression, 47, 54, 57, 63, 68, 70, 79, 156
Derbyshire, 62
Detroit, 38
Domville, Admiral Sir Barry, 135
Dorman, Geoffrey, 87
Dublin, 10, 25, 149
Dundas, Ian Hope, 84, 96, 98
Dunkirk, 134
Durham Miners' Gala, 45

Eccles, Colonel, 13
education, 17
Edward VIII, King, *see* Windsor, Duke of
Eichmann, Adolf, 150
Elizabeth I, Queen, 2
Elliott, Maxine, 15
Elliott, Walter, 51, 54
England, *see* Britain
English Array, 100
English Mystery, 100
Euphorion Books, 146
European, The, 152, 153
European Union, 146
Evening Standard, 62, 88

Fabre-Luce, Lottsie, 62–3
Fairbanks, Douglas, 42
Fasces, 67, 72, 113
fascist movements, 52, 55, 58, 67–8, 72, 83–4
Fascist Quarterly, 95
fencing, 7, 69–70, 72
First World War, 10, 67, 68, 107, 137, 139
Flanders, 11, 52
Florida, 38
Foreign Office, 14

Forgan, Robert, 54–5, 63, 83
Fox, Charles James, 139
France, 55, 61, 97, 104, 149–50, 152, 156; fascism, 67; revolutionary, 139; at war, 132, 134
Franco, General Francisco, 103
French Riviera, 41, 42, 46, 57, 62
Freud, Sigmund, 5, 127
Fuller, Major-General J F C 'Boney', 88, 110–11

Gaiety Girls, 8
Game, Sir Philip, 115
Gandhi, Mahatma, 35
Garvin, James, 26, 54
General Strike, 39
George V, King, 21, 31, 63
Germans, 12
Germany, 43, 69, 97, 149; broadcasts from, 99; capitulation, 144; fascism, 67–8; Hitler comes to power, 70; industry, 55; Nazi, 52, 102–3, 118–19, 125, 128–30, 143; post-war, 144, 151; threat of war, 104–5, 107, 109, 129
Glasgow, 64
Glasgow, Earl of, 97
Glyn, Elinor, 22
Gobineau, Count, 67
Goebbels, Joseph, 107, 108, 116–18
Goebbels, Magda, 108, 116–17
Goethe, Johann Wolfgang von, 135, 145–6
Gordon-Canning, Captain, 117
Grandi, Count Dino, 89, 95–6
Grey, C J, 87
Guest, Colonel Freddie, 16
Guildford, 23
Guinness, Bryan, 74, 80, 144
Guinness, Desmond, 75
Guinness, Diana (née Mitford), *see* Mosley, Diana
Guinness, Jonathan, 75

Halifax, Lord, 139
Ham Common, 138
Hamilton, Gerald, 144
Hamm, Jeffrey, 153, 155
Hanfstängel, 'Putzi', 104–5, 126
Harmsworth, Alfred, 4
Harrow, 16, 30, 32, 34, 38, 55; Conservative Association, 27–8
Haw-Haw, Lord, *see* Joyce William
Hawkins, Neil Francis, 72, 83, 91, 113
Hazebrouck, 13
Heathcote family, 4
Henderson, Arthur, 44
Hickson, Oswald, 133
Higgs, Nanny, 40, 142
Hitler, Adolf, 15, 83, 91, 104–8, 110, 122, 138;

INDEX 179

comes to power, 70, 80; death, 79; Mosley copies tactics, 85–6; interviews with, 98; agrees to Mosley broadcasts, 99, 125; involvement in Spanish Civil War, 103; notion of womanhood, 105; meets Mosley, 106–7; 'feminine charm', 107; sense of humour, 107; pact with Stalin, 109; guest of honour at Mosley's wedding, 116–17; oratory, 117; his circle, 125–6; moves towards war, 128; suicide, 144; described in *My Life*, 156; Mosley's final verdict, 157

Hitler–Stalin pact, 109

Holocaust, 106, 147, 150

Hore-Belisha, Leslie, 41, 51, 57

Hough End, 2

Houston, Lady Lucy, 61, 98

Howard, Peter, 58, 64

Huxley, Aldous, 91

Huyton, 139

Iddesleigh, Earl of, 87

Ileclash, 152

immigration, 102–3, 153

Imperial Fascist League (IFL), 71, 73, 100, 135

Inchape, Lord, 97

Independent Labour Party, 42, 80, 84, 137

India, 19, 35, 40, 57

internment, 138

IRA, 25, 26

Ireland, 24–6, 28, 71, 99, 149–50

Isfield, Sussex, 23

Isherwood, Christopher, 65, 144

Isle of Man, 139

Italy, 81, 96, 97, 111, 138, 149–51; fascism, 67–70, 89–90, 153; invasion of Abyssinia, 103

Jackson, Derek, 141, 142

James, Henry, 19

Jameson, Storm, 91

Jaurès, Jean, 130

Jebb, Gladwyn, 135

Jews, 71–2, 78, 94, 101–2, 108, 113–14, 122–4, 127; businessmen, 93; in Communist Party, 112; in East End, 85, 102, 104; fighting fascists, 112, 115, 138, 148; pogroms, 128; politicians, 41, 51, 57; threatened with expulsion, 114, 123; in Vienna, 128; and war, 105, 129; *see also* anti-Semitism

Joad, C E M, 57, 58, 60, 61

John Bull, 4

John, Augustus, 75, 76

Joyce, William (Lord Haw-Haw), 84, 96, 101–3, 113, 120–1; leaves BUF, 98; wartime activities, 99, 131; sacked from BU, 122–3

Junger, Ernst, 151

Kent, Tyler, 132

Keynes, John Maynard, 30, 35, 44; biography, 34; endorses 'Mosley memorandum', 48

Kitchener, Lord, 19

Kohl, Helmut, 151

Kristallnacht, 128

Labour Party, 18, 24, 29, 40, 84–5, 138; Mosley joins, 31, 32–5, 68, 71; government collapses, 34–5; Mosley's popularity within, 39, 42; 1929 election and aftermath, 44–5, 47–56; 'Mosley memorandum', 48–9, 50; 'Mosley Manifesto', 54; 'New Labour Group', 54; Mosley expelled, 56; launched at Farringdon Memorial Hall, 56, 78; opposition to New Party, 57–9, 64; 'National Labour', 63; 1931 election, 65; 1935 election, 102; London County Council elections, 122; in wartime coalition, 140; 1945 government, 147

Ladywood, 34, 44

Lamb, Henry, 76

Lancashire, 1, 58, 86

Lansbury, George, 45, 139

League of Nations, 24, 29, 103

League of Youth and Social Progress, 19

Leeds, 85

Leese, Arnold, 71, 73, 100, 135, 153

Leicestershire, 15, 21

Leiter, Mary, 19–20, 26

Lewis, Kid, 64

Liberals, 15, 18, 24, 25; approach to Mosley, 16; in decline, 29, 31; bring down Ramsay MacDonald's government, 34; 1929 election and aftermath, 44–5, 54; split, 57; in National Government, 63

Liddell Hart, Basil, 87

Link, the, 126

Linton-Orman, Rotha, 72, 83

Liverpool, 85, 120, 124; prison, 133

Llandudno, 53

Lloyd, Geoffrey, 91

Lloyd, Lord, 87, 97

Lloyd George, David, 14, 16, 25–6, 80, 138; biography, 15; coalition falls, 28, 52; War Cabinet, 48; radicalism, 44, 57; approaches to Mosley, 61, 70, 79; excluded from National Government, 63; distrust of Mosley, 88; defends and sympathises with Mosley, 92–3; praise for Hitler, 106; opposition to Boer War, 139; described in *My Life*, 156

Lloyd George, Megan, 80

London, 4, 5, 15–16, 23, 101; Blitz, 136; Brixton prison, 133, 135, 136, 139; Cable Street, 114–16, 118; Cannon Street Hotel, 60; Dolphin Square, 131, 133; Earl's Court, 129; East End, 64, 85, 102–4, 112–15, 118, 121–2, 147–8, 152, 155;

Eaton Square, 80; Ebury Street, 75, 77; Farringdon Memorial Hall, 56, 78, 147; Friends' Meeting House, 80; Great George Street, 60, 73; Great Smith Street, 111; Harrods, 137; Holloway prison, 133, 134, 137, 139–41; Mile End Road, 118; Notting Hill, 153–4; Olympia, 90–3, 98, 101–2, 116; Ritz Hotel, 16; Royal Albert Hall, 89–90, 101, 113; St James's Palace, 21; Smith Square, 23; Trafalgar Square, 78, 155; West End, 8, 136

London County Council, 118; elections, 113, 121, 123, 124

Loos, 13

Low Countries, 132

Lutyens, Sir Edwin, 81

MacDonald, James Ramsay, 25, 31–2, 34, 42–50, 52; biography, 42; heads National Government, 61, 63; opposition to First World War, 139

Macmillan, Harold, 51; supports 'Mosley Manifesto', 54

McNab, John, 123

Madagascar, 114

Magnus, Philip, 87

Manchester, 2, 3; Free Trade Hall, 85

Market Drayton, Shropshire, 4, 6

Marks and Spencer, 79

Marsh, Eddie, 76

Marx, Karl, 68, 127

Mary, Queen, 21

Mary, Queen of Scots, 2

Maugham, Somerset, 42

Maury, Paula Casa, 46

Maxton, James (Jimmy), 42, 80, 137

May Committee, 62, 63

Mengele, Josef, 150

Metcalfe, 'Fruity', 79, 120

Metcalfe, Baba (née Lady Alexandra Curzon), 20, 46, 81, 120; nickname, 79; affair with Mosley, 79, 83, 85, 104, 111, 157; affair with Grandi, 89, 95; travels to Germany, 105; visits Mosley in prison, 136; pleads Mosley's case, 139

MI5, 57, 83, 93, 96, 110, 117, 122, 132, 138

Middleton, Lord, 87

Mikardo, Ian, 65

Ministry of Munitions, 14

Mitchison, Naomi, 91

Mitford, Deborah, 149

Mitford, Diana, see Mosley, Diana

Mitford, Jessica, see Romilly, Jessica

Mitford, Nancy, 126; demands Mosleys' internment, 135, 141

Mitford, Pamela, 134, 141, 149

Mitford, Tom, 106, 126; joins forces, 131; pleads Mosley's case, 139

Mitford, Unity, 80, 104–8, 117, 127; interferes in Hitler's circle, 125–6; shoots herself, 130; death, 148

Mitterrand, François, 151

modernism, 1

Molotov, Vyacheslav, 109

Monckton, Walter, 136

Mond, Henry, 51

Monnet, Jean, 146

Montague, Margaret, 15

Monte Carlo, 150

Moreau, General, 150

Morning Post, 53

Morris, Hugh, 30

Morris, Sir William, 55, 62, 97

Morrison, Herbert, 32, 39, 47, 49, 118; and Mosleys' internment, 136, 138, 139–40

Mosley, Alexander, 130, 149, 153; education, 143

Mosley, Cynthia (Cimmie) (née Curzon), 19–21; marriage, 21–2, 26, 46, 76, 157; breach with father, 26; and Mosley's infidelities, 26, 42, 46, 62–3, 76–7; popularity with Labour Party, 33; visits US, 38; attacked in press, 40; elected in Stoke-on-Trent, 44–5; signs 'Mosley Manifesto', 54; leaves Labour, 55–6; in New Party, 58–60; pregnancy and illness, 63, 65, 69, 71, 76; disapproval of fascism, 68; remains loyal, 78; illness and death, 80–2, 85, 104; accused of being Jewish, 100

Mosley, Diana (formerly Guinness, née Mitford), 74–81, 83, 89, 104, 111; divorce, 80; travels to Germany and meets Hitler, 99, 104–8, 112, 130; learns German, 104–5; engagement and marriage, 106, 108, 116–18, 130; injured in car accident, 111; abortion, 112; biography of Wallis Simpson, 121; argues with Nicholas, 125; offended by Nancy Mitford's book, 127; children born to Mosley, 130, 131; seeks legal help against internment, 133; interned, 134–5, 137, 139–41; under restrictions, 142; home-making, 143–4; translations of Balzac, 146; in exile from Britain, 149; edits *The European*, 152; edits *My Life*, 156; unwilling to criticise fascist past, 157; death, 157

Mosley, Edward, 2–3

Mosley, John, 4

Mosley, Katherine Maud (née Heathcote), 4–5, 6; enthusiasm for fascism, 78, 83, 86; calls in royal physician, 140; death, 148

Mosley, Max, 131, 134, 149, 155; education, 143

Mosley, Michael (Micky), 71, 76, 125; under aunt's guardianship, 134, 144

Mosley, Nicholas, 2

Mosley, Nicholas, 5, 80, 108, 140; born, 23; childhood, 40, 41, 125; describes Mosley's speeches, 89, 154; on Wootton Lodge, 112; argues with Diana, 125; breach with Mosley, 153–5; reconciled, 156–7

Mosley, Oswald (great-great-grandfather), 3

Mosley, Oswald (grandfather), 4, 5, 6; relationship with grandson, 4, 6, 10; sets up trust fund, 8; death, 21

Mosley, Oswald (father), 4–5; death, 33, 40, 43

Mosley, Oswald Ernald: claims of ancestry, 1, 4; birth, 4; relationship with grandfather, 4, 6, 10; account of his father, 5; relationship with mother, 5; childhood, 6; nicknamed Tom, 6; cruelty and violence, 6–9, 15, 41; education, 6–7; beneficiary of trust fund, 8; First World War experiences, 10–13; contempt for death, 11; admiration for German enemy, 12; developing fascism, 12, 37, 54, 55, 59–61, 64, 68–74, 78–80; injured leg, 13–15; self-education, 14; mistresses, 15; enters politics as Conservative, 15–19; first manifesto, 16–17; inheritance, 21; marriage with Cimmie, 21–2, 26, 46, 76, 157; campaign over Ireland, 24–6; leaves Tories and sits as Independent MP, 24, 28–30, 68, 71; infidelities, 26, 42, 46, 62–3, 76–7, 79, 153; litigation, 28, 124, 127, 137; joins Labour, 31, 68, 71; lifestyle, 32–3, 37, 40–3, 62, 69, 72, 111; socialism, 35–7, 68; 'Birmingham proposals', 35; 'Revolution by Reason', 35, 37; failure to understand human nature, 37; visits US, 38; as parent, 41–2; rudeness, 42; in Labour government and 'Mosley Memorandum', 45–9, 50; resigns from government, 50–1; anti-Semitism, 51, 78–9, 99–100, 102, 113, 123, 138, 154; battle within Labour Party and 'Mosley Manifesto', 51–6; leaves Labour, 55–6; heads New Party, 56–61, 63–5, 71; excluded from National Government, 63; defeated in Stoke, 65; meets Mussolini, 70, 80, 96, 111; 'The Greater Britain', 72, 76; founds BUF, 72–3, 77, 83–8; meets Diana, 74–7; and Cimmie's death, 80–3, 85; as 'The Leader', 83; ill health, 89, 140–1, 143; adopts Italian trappings, 90; move towards Nazism, 90, 99, 131; finances BUF and BU, 96–7, 142; radio schemes, 98–9, 108, 125; meets Hitler, 106–7, 117; engagement and marriage with Diana, 106, 108, 112, 116–18, 130; changes movement's name, 113; and 'King's party' idea, 120; distanced from BU organisation, 122; injured in Liverpool, 124; offended by Nancy Mitford's book, 127; *Tomorrow We Live*, 127; declares loyalty, 131–2; interned, 133, 135–41; learns German, 135; interrogated, 138; joins Diana in Holloway, 139–40; under restrictions, 142; proclaims new beliefs and launches Union Movement, 145–8; *My Answer*, 145; *The Alternative*, 145, 147, 151; in exile from Britain, 149; founds *The European*, 152; breach with Nicholas, 153–5; last election campaigns, 154, 155; publishes *My Life*, 156; reconciled with Nicholas, 156–7; criticism of fascist past, 157; last illness and death, 157

Mosley, Ted, 4, 43

Mosley, Tonman, 4

Mosley, Vivien, 23; childhood, 40, 41, 125; under aunt's guardianship, 134

Mosley family, 1–4; motto, 2

Movimento Soziale Italiano, 151

Muggeridge, Malcolm, 156

Munich, 105, 118, 130; 'Brown House', 85; conference, 128

Mussolini, Benito, 53, 67, 72, 83, 138, 151; biography, 52; Mosley meets, 70, 80, 96, 111; Rothermere meets, 88; support for BUF, 95–6; involvement in Spanish Civil War, 103; Hitler imitates, 107; joins war, 136; murdered, 144; rescued after ousting, 150

Napoleon Bonaparte, 23

National Council for Civil Liberties, 112

National Government, 61, 63–5, 70, 102–3, 118, 120

nationalism, 17, 145

Nazism, 90, 99, 100, 103, 106, 151

New Members Parliamentary Committee, 18

New Party, 56–65, 68, 71, 83, 95; 'Biff Boys', 58, 60; launched at Farringdon Memorial Hall, 56, 78, 147; marigold emblem, 58, 64; Youth Movement, 60, 71; uniforms, 64; *Crisis* film barred, 65

New Statesman, 50

New York, 38

News Chronicle, 124

Nicolson, Harold, 41, 49, 51; supports 'Mosley Manifesto', 54; funding, 55, 62, 97; in New Party, 57, 58, 60, 62, 63–5; warns Mosley against fascism, 69, 79; parts with Mosley, 70; distaste for fascism, 78; visits Mosley in prison, 137

Nietzsche, Friedrich, 23, 67, 135, 145–6

Night of the Long Knives, 105, 123

Nordic League, 100, 126

Nuremberg rallies, 104–5, 112

Observer, 26, 54

O'Connor, T J, 92

Odessa, 150

Okhrana, 100

Orsay, 149, 157

Owen, Cunliffe, 97

Oxford Union, 152

pacifism, 104, 109, 128–31, 135
Page, Walter, 22
Palestine, 114, 148
Paris, 4, 41, 121, 149–50; Père-Lachaise cemetery, 157
Partridge, Bernard, 54
patriotism, 90, 95, 121, 139, 145
Peace with Ireland Council, 25
Pemberton, Max, 98
Pennsylvania, 38
pensions, 46, 48
Perón, Juan, 150
Petrie, Sir Charles, 87, 97
Philby, Harry St John, 135
Pickering, Vernon, 87
Pirow, Oswald, 147
Plato, 145
Plymouth, 20
Poland, 109, 129
polo, 8–9
Portal, Lord, 97
Portofino, 22, 23
Portugal, 149
Pound, Ezra, 152
Prague, 100
Price, G Ward, 98
protectionism, 19, 30, 47, 53–4, 104
'Protocols of the Elders of Zion', 100
Provence, 89
Prussian Guards, 13
Public Order Bill and Act, 118–19, 124
Punch, 54

Quisling, Vidkun, 132

racism, 147, 153–4
radio, 98–9, 108, 125
Ramsay, Archibald Maule, 132–3, 135
Redesdale, Lord and Lady, 74; converted to fascism, 106, 126
Ribbentrop, Joachim von, 109
Richardson, Mary, 86
Riefenstahl, Leni, 104, 105
Right Club, 126, 132–3
Rignell, 141
Roe, E Mandeville, 72
Roe, Sir Alliott Verdon, 87, 97
Rolleston, Staffordshire, 2, 4, 5, 6, 23
Rome, 69, 80, 88, 111
Romilly, Esmond, 126, 141
Romilly, Jessica (née Mitford), 126, 141
Roosevelt, Franklin D, 38, 132–3; New Deal, 34, 48, 79, 80; biography, 79; described in *My Life*, 156

Ross, Colin, 110
Rothermere, Lord, 68, 88, 98; withdraws support from BUF, 93–4, 101–3, 110
Royal Flying Corps (RFC), 10–11, 87
Rudel, Hans-Ulrich, 146
Russell of Liverpool, Lord, 87
Russia, 109; Bolshevik revolution, 14, 68, 100; Civil War, 24

Sackville-West, Vita, 64
Sandhurst, 7–9, 10
Sark, 99
Sassoon, Sir Philip, 74
Savehay Farm (Denham), 40, 59
Schiller, Friedrich, 135
Schuman, Robert, 146
Scotland, 134
Scrimgeour, Alex, 97
Scrymgeour-Wedderburn, J, 92
Second World War, 24, 121
Selsey, Sussex, 87, 125
Shinwell, Emmanuel, 59
Shipton-under-Wychwood, 142
Shoreham, Sussex, 12
Shropshire, 4, 5
Sieff, Israel, 79
Simon, Sir John, 25, 29, 57, 115
Simpson, Mrs Wallis, 74, 119, 121
Sinclair, Archibald, 51, 61
Sitwell, Georgia, 42, 78
Sitwell, Osbert, 78
Sitwell, Sacheverell, 41
Skidelsky, Robert, 6, 54
Skorzeny, Otto, 150
Smethwick, 39, 40, 45, 55
Smith F E, 15, 28, 32
Snowden, Philip, 39, 44, 46–7, 49, 50; biography, 47; joins National Government, 63
Sorrento, 113
Sousa, John Philip, 78
South Africa, 146
South Wales, 85, 119
Soviet Union, 61, 109
Spaak, Paul Henri, 146
Spain, 149–50
Spanish Civil War, 103, 121, 126
Spears, Brigadier-General Sir Edward, 87
Spectator, 35
Spencer, Stanley, 76
Spengler, Oswald, 67
Squire, Sir John, 87
SS, 150–1; uniform style, 113
Staffordshire, 1–4, 6, 16, 44, 112
Stalin, Joseph, 95; pact with Hitler, 109

Stanley, Oliver, 51
Stoke-on-Trent, 44, 65
Stone, Staffordshire, 16
Strachey, John, 38, 42, 44, 49, 51; 'Revolution by Reason', 35, 37; helps compile 'Mosley Manifesto', 54; leaves Labour to join New Party, 55–6; in New Party, 58–61; resigns, 61
Strachey, Lytton, 35, 75
Sudetenland, 128
Sunday Dispatch, 88
Sunday Express, 52
Sunday Pictorial, 92
Suner, Ramon Serrano, 150
Sussex, 85

Taverner, Mary Russell, 104
Taylor, A J P, 156
Taylour, 'Fabulous' Fay, 87
Teddy Boys, 153
Temple de la Gloire, 150
Thomas, J H, 44–5, 47–9, 63
Thomson, Alexander Raven, 84, 114, 121–2, 138, 147
Time & Tide, 61, 98
Times, The, 51, 68, 92
Tollemache, Baron, 97
Tories (Conservatives), 4, 18, 28–9, 31–2, 34; Mosley joins, 16–17; Mosley leaves, 24, 49, 52, 68; 1929 election and aftermath, 44–5, 52, 54; win Ashton-under-Lyme, 59; in National Government, 63
trade unions, 53
Tutbury Castle, 2–3

unemployment, 15, 30, 43–6, 48, 51, 84; benefit, 62–3
Union Movement, 147–8, 152–5
United States of America, 38, 61, 127; economy, 79, 80; industry, 55; intervention in war, 132–3; power of, 14

Venice, 37, 41, 72, 74, 76, 150
Vienna, 128
Virgil, 146

Wagner, Richard, 107, 125, 130
Wagner, Winifred, 107
Wales, Prince of, 74
Wall Street Crash, 47, 62
war, 12, 19, 29, 43; total, 14
Ward, Dudley, 45
Ward-Jackson, Major, 28
Waugh, Evelyn, 75
Webb, Beatrice, 27, 35, 41, 48
Webb, Sidney, 35
Webster, Nesta, 71
Wegg-Prosser, Charles, 124
Wertheimer, Egon, 33
West Downs school, 6–7
Whigs, 3
Whitelands, 85
Williams-Ellis, Clough, 41
Williamson, Henry, 87, 152
Winchester College, 7, 87
Windsor, Duke of, 106, 139, 150; abdication crisis, 119–21
Wodehouse, P G, 127
Wolkoff, Anna, 132
women, 14; attracted to Mosley, 15; join BUF, 86
Woolf, Leonard, 25
Wootton Lodge, 112, 121, 125, 127, 131, 143

Yeats-Brown, Major Francis, 87
Young, Allan, 44, 54; in New Party, 58–60; resigns, 61
Younger, Sir George, 16
Ypres, 11; second Battle of, 12, 13

LIFE & TIMES FROM HAUS

Churchill
by S. Haffner
'One of the most brilliant things of any length ever written about Churchill.' *TLS*
1-904341-07-1 (pb)
1-904341-06-3 (hb)
£9.99 (pb) £12.99 (hb)

Curie
by S. Dry
'...this book could hardly be bettered' *New Scientist*
selected as Outstanding Academic Title by *Choice*
1-904341-29-2
£9.99 (pb)

Dietrich
by M. Skaerved
'It is probably the best book ever on Marlene.' C. Downes
1-904341-13-6 (pb)
1-904341-12-8 (hb)
£9.99 (pb) £12.99 (hb)

Einstein
by P.D. Smith
'Concise, complete, well-produced and lively throughout, ... a bargain at the price.' *New Scientist*
1-904341-15-2 (pb)
1-904341-14-4 (hb)
£9.99 (pb) £12.99 (hb)

Beethoven
by M. Geck
'...this little gem is a truly handy reference.' *Musical Opinion*
1-904341-00-4 (pb)
1-904341-03-9 (hb)
£9.99 (pb) £12.99 (hb)

Casement
by A. Mitchell
'hot topic' *The Irish Times*
1-904341-41-1
£9.99 (pb)

Prokofiev
by T. Schipperges
'beautifully made, . . . well-produced photographs, . . . with useful historical nuggets.' *The Guardian*
1-904341-32-2 (pb)
1-904341-34-9 (hb)
£9.99 (pb) £12.99 (hb)

Britten
by D. Matthews
'I have read them all - but none with as much enjoyment as this.' *Literary Review*
1-904341-21-7 (pb)
1-904341-39-X (hb)
£9.99 (pb) £12.99 (hb)

De Gaulle
by J. Jackson
'this concise and distinguished book' Andrew Roberts *Sunday Telegraph*
1-904341-44-6
£9.99 (pb)

Dostoevsky
by R. Freeborn
'... wonderful ... a learned guide' *The Sunday Times*
1-904341-27-6 (pb)
£9.99 (pb)

Orwell
by S. Lucas
'short but controversial assessment ... is sure to raise a few eyebrows' *Sunday Tasmanian*
1-904341-33-0
£9.99 (pb)

Brahms
by H. Neunzig
'readable, comprehensive and attractively priced'
The Irish Times
1-904341-17-9 (pb)
£9.99 (pb)

Bach
by M. Geck
'The production values of the book are exquisite, too.'
The Guardian
1-904341-16-0 (pb)
1-904341-35-7 (hb)
£9.99 (pb) £12.99 (hb)

Verdi
by B. Meier
'These handy volumes fill a gap in the market ... admirably.'
Classic fM
1-904341-05-5 (pb)
1-904341-04-7 (hb)
£9.99 (pb) £12.99 (hb)

Kafka
by K. Wagenbach
'One of the most useful books about Kafka ever published' *Frankfurter Allgemeine Zeitung*
1-904341-02-0 (pb)
1-904341-01-2 (hb)
£9.99 (pb) £12.99 (hb)

Armstrong
by D. Bradbury
'generously illustrated ... a fine and well-researched introduction' George Melly
Daily Mail
1-904341-46-2 (pb)
1-904341-47-0 (hb)
£9.99 (pb) £12.99 (hb)